Things to Do with Toddlers and Twos

Things to Do with Toddlers and Twos

Written and illustrated by
KAREN MILLER

International Standard Book Number 0–910287–04–X

TENTH PRINTING

Written and Illustrated by Karen Miller

Table of Contents

Dedication

This book is dedicated to Dr. Grace Mitchell, an inspiring woman, who has dedicated her life to serving children well, improving the child care profession and helping adults understand children.

Acknowledgments

The seeds for this book were planted when I was asked to present a workshop on curriculum for toddlers at a state conference of the Colorado Association for the Education of Young Children. I immediately called my friend and respected colleague, Jo Layfield who is a Center Director for Children's World. We spent two week-ends brainstorming at Jo's cabin in the mountains and the resulting workshop handout became the outline for this book. I thank Jo for her many pragmatic ideas and her "catalytic action", as well as her proofreading services.

I am grateful also to Lois Dewsnap for her editing help.

The many teachers in Children's World centers have given invaluable input of ideas and feedback on what works. I would like to give special thanks to Patti Ohl, Mary Bulloch, Verlene Kreider, Pat Romano, and Pauline Myers who have been especially helpful in sharing ideas.

I wish to express thanks also to the students in the child development class I taught at the Community College of Denver, most of whom are family day care providers, for giving me the perspective of their environment. Special thanks to Mary Bedoya, Pat Olmstead, Mary Broussard, Raye Silverman, Karen McLaughlin and Evelyn Vernon.

I would also like to acknowledge some major influences on my own learning.

Dr. Burton White's two-day institute, "Educating the Infant and Toddler" which he offers on a continuing basis in cities around the country, offered a wealth of useful information about early development in a very short time, providing me with many starting points for further study.

Dr. Alice Honig through Syracuse University offers week-long summer seminars in infants and toddlers, giving participants strong theoretical exposure and examination of important research. This experience was stimulating and valuable.

I must also acknowledge the influence of my teachers at Pacific Oaks College and in particular Polly McVickar who taught me so much about the processes of imagination and creativity in young children and adults.

Introduction

Toddlers are learners. They seem to spend every waking moment trying to figure out how the world works. As they develop new skills like climbing or walking, they have to find out just how far that skill will take them, and practice it over and over again.

They make the wonderful discovery that when a certain sequence of sounds comes out of their mouths just right it is likely to get a particular desired response. How fascinating, that everything seems to have a combination of certain sounds! Language!

Toddlers spend much of their time uncovering the "mechanics" of every day living. They are fascinated by gravity. They have learned and continue to test the fact that things fall down, not up, when dropped. In addition, things usually make some sort of noise when they hit something else. And there is such a variety of noises to discover!

The properties of water fascinate children. Water pours down, but splashes up. Funny bubbles make funny noises. Water assumes different shapes when poured into different containers. With water, toddlers can make things happen!

Principles of leverage are interesting to toddlers. (Elementary physics at its most elementary!) They discover the leverage of their own body when they climb and pull themselves up on things. The pages of a book, cabinet doors, the handle on the toilet, a rocking chair, all are things to be investigated.

The toddler also spends much time exploring the relationships of space and volume: What fits into what ... what will support what ... how objects relate to each other. Toys that have pieces that fit together, and toys that nest or stack attract much interest from toddlers.

My motivation for writing this book originated with the problems and requests for help from adults who work with toddlers in group child care situations. As I presented my ideas to various groups of people, I learned that it was not just child care center caregivers who were interested in activities for toddlers. I found equal interest from family day care providers, play group supervisors, babysitters, and parents who are trying to provide toddlers with a stimulating environment in which to grow and learn. So, although at times this book may address specific situations of toddlers in group care, it is really written for anyone who is looking for ideas and activities that do not merely "occupy" a toddler, but also stimulate the child's natural curiosity and development of intelligence.

As I observed many people working with toddlers in different settings, I noticed that successful teachers and parents seemed "tuned in" to the toddlers. They were able to pick up and expand upon what the children do naturally, building upon children's interests rather than constantly restricting and prohibiting them, while at the same time setting consistent and appropriate limits. They were not so much preoccupied with "teaching" children and cramming endless facts into their young heads as they were in sharing in a child's joy of discovery. They encouraged, arbitrated, explained and demonstrated a knack for providing just the right challenge to the young explorers.

At several points in the book I refer to "the envelope of language". This term simply means to surround the child with meaningful language to enhance the learning value of the experience.

It's one thing to present a child with a fingerpainting project, say, but it becomes all the more valuable when the adult talks about the color of the paint, the texture, the designs the child is producing, etc. Talking about the wind and the weather when outside enhances the outdoor experience. The "envelope of language" is particularly important in the infant and toddler years.

Not just any talk is a valid and valuable "envelope of language". Babies who have spent long hours in front of television sets show no gains in language development; in fact, they often show a significant lag. It has to be real language with a real human being. And even that is not quite enough. To be meaningful to an infant or toddler, the talk must be about the "here and now". Talk about what the child sees in front of his eyes, what he and you are doing at the moment, what he can perceive with his senses. That's when language connects in the brain of a very young child. Describe what you are doing, or what the child is doing: "Jennifer is swinging back and forth, back and forth." Get into the habit of talking to yourself. "Okay, now I'm setting the table . . . one plate here, one plate there, a glass here, and a glass there. Oh, there's the telephone ringing. I better answer it." It sounds rather idiotic to other adults, but "self talk" is good for the language development of children in your presence. Providing clear, descriptive language to accompany children's real every day experiences is the best way to "teach" concepts such as color, size, and shape rather than sitting children down for a "lesson".

When I talk about "toddlers" in this book, I am referring to children roughly between the ages of 12 months and about 3 years of age. There are toys and activities described that will appeal to younger and older children as well. The child of 12 or 13 months who is just learning to "toddle" is very different from the competent human being of 36 months. The learning and development that takes place in this 24 month span of time is really phenomenal. One of the most exciting things about working with toddlers is that they seem to be changing every day, and indeed they are! Knowing what interests children, what they can and cannot do, and what they are just ready to do will help in planning activities that will enhance children's development and minimize frustration on the part of the adult and the child.

I have resisted applying specific age guidelines to the activities described in this book. I would rather have the adult "go by intuition" and try to sense what the child can do. You will know immediately if you guessed wrong, and can either simplify the activity or drop it and try something else. Most of the activities have a rather broad range of appeal and children will perform tasks according to their own level of skill. In the appendix are several books listed which have developmental charts of skills and interests if you feel a need for that.

I have chosen to organize the material in this book according to the different types of toddler *behaviors*. In my observations I focused on what toddlers really *do* most of the time. I noticed that there are certain behaviors that toddlers seem to do over and over again, and you can expect these same behaviors in any toddler. At times I felt that these actions (sticking fingers in holes, climbing, etc.) seemed almost compulsive . . . nature seemed to require that they do it. Believing that toddlers are natural learners, I felt that their compulsive behaviors must have some purpose in their overall learning and development. It usually didn't take too much searching to find the learning value in their natural activities.

An interesting learning phenomenon to be aware of when working with toddlers is the "emerging skills compulsion", or "mastery behavior" as it is sometimes called. Everyone experiences this, not just toddlers. Whenever a person acquires a new skill, especially something that was difficult or challenging to learn, the person has a compulsion to practice it again and again and again. This might be part of the appeal of video games. Think of the teenager who first learns to drive a car. He can't get enough of it. How about the six year old who learns to whistle. She'll drive you crazy for awhile! The student who learns to play a song on the guitar will play it over and over again. "Self imposed drill" seems to be a natural way for people to solidify what they learn. Toddlers are picking up many, many new skills and understandings and they have to practice and test them over and over again. We who work with children of this age need to recognize this and give them many opportunities to practice their newly acquired capabilities.

A widely recognized principle of behavior management in the profession of early childhood education is that of "positive redirection". What this really amounts to is looking at whatever negative or undesirable behavior a child is involved in, finding the closest activity that *is* acceptable and getting the child involved in that instead. For example, if a child is banging on the window with a cup the teacher can give her a drum to bang on instead; if the child is climbing on bookshelves, the teacher can direct the child to the climber. The child can still practice the compulsion. This principle won't always work, but often it will help. This book is full of possible "positive redirection" activities.

I have included many simple inexpensive homemade toys to make. Of the many places where I have observed toddlers, it was not always in the settings where there were the most expensive and plentiful commercial toys that I found the best program. When a teacher or parent takes the time to make a toy, it is special. Many of the ideas for toys came from gifted teachers who generously shared their idea. Some are adaptations of concepts seen in commercial toys. A few are pure fabrications from my imagination. All, however, have been tested with children in group and home situations and have proven their worth by attracting the concentration and attention of toddlers.

I will occasionally name a commercial toy that fits a purpose particularly well.

Safety is always a concern when working with very young children. Their physical instability, combined with their exploratory nature and their compulsion to put everything in their mouth requires that toddlers be closely supervised at all times. I have added a safety note whenever a toy or activity could present an obvious potential danger. Toddlers, however, can manage to hurt themselves on just about anything! It is extremely important to "babyproof" your environment, removing common hazards. Put safety plugs in all electrical outlets when not in use, make sure poisonous substances are not stored where children can get into them, check to make sure plants are not poisonous, get safety latches for cabinet doors and drawers, make sure hot water from faucets cannot get too hot, stabilize tippy furniture or remove it, make sure outdoor areas are adequately fenced, keep sharp objects out of reach, do not keep medication in your purse, etc. Most important — maintain an awareness — stay alert to any possible hazard.

In order to simplify writing style I randomly refer to children as male or female when gender is specified. There is no intended preference.

This book is not meant to be an in-depth discussion of child development. For that I refer you to the annotated bibliography of resources I have found useful. Rather, it is a compilation of ideas gathered from respected colleagues in the child care profession and skillful parents I have talked to ... people who have a "knack" for having fun with toddlers.

Since this is a book about activities and not "how to run a good child care program", I do not discuss the critical issues of diaper changing, potty training, hygiene, nutrition, behavior problems, separation and adjustment, parent involvement and other concerns of group care. Again, I refer you to the annotated bibliography.

Finally, I do not intend to suggest that doing all the activities in this book will insure a child of superior intelligence. However, an awful lot of learning takes place between a child's first and third birthdays. It is a critical time for developing a firm foundation for intellectual development. If you are looking for ways to make the time you spend with toddlers more pleasant and interesting for *both* you and the children, this book can help you. Respect your toddlers—they are wonderful and at an exciting stage of development. Let them be all they can be by knowing how to work with their natural learning drives, within a secure framework of limits and routines, rather than working against them.

Most of all, relax and have fun with it all!

Things to Do with Toddlers and Twos

CHAPTER 1

Cause and Effect

"I wonder what would happen if ..." seems to be the constant unspoken question in toddlers' minds. They have discovered that they can make things happen. Power! We see this in their fascination with switching lights on and off, unrolling toilet paper, flushing toilets, ringing doorbells and knocking things over. Actually this process is the beginning of logical thought: action A causes response B. Our little scientists will test actions over and over to see if they produce the same results.

You and I would probably do the same thing if we were suddenly placed on a new planet. In order to act as independent beings we have to figure out how the world works so we can rely on ourselves and not forever be dependent on others. Besides, making things happen is fun!

Toddlers are fascinated by getting dramatic results from simple hand actions. It's especially interesting if a sound consequence accompanies the effect.

Play Ball!

Toddlers are fascinated by all kinds of balls. Any kind of ball play is a good "cause and effect" activity because an action produces an immediate response. Vary the action, the response varies.

Show a small group of children or an individual child how to roll the ball back and forth with you. They will enjoy the social give and take as well as the action of the ball.

Kicking a ball is a real challenge for toddlers because they have to balance on one foot to kick with the other foot. What pride when they can finally do it!

More Ball Challenges:

Ask: " What else can you use to make the ball move? Can you bump the ball with your elbow? Try your knee."

A Ball Collection

A good collection of different sizes of balls is fairly inexpensive and will be much enjoyed by your toddlers. The popular foam rubber balls are great for indoor play but toddlers like to bite chunks out of them, so keep a watchful eye. Tennis balls, a beach ball, a foot ball, and large rubber balls make a good collection. Keep them in a large laundry basket, or a large decorated cardboard box to facilitate clean-up.

Ball Through a Tube

A tennis ball and a large cardboard giftwrap tube or a mailing tube work well for this. Toddlers love to stick the ball in one end and see it come shooting out the other end. Attach the tube to a stair railing with a basket to receive the ball at the end.

Marbles in a Tube

Get some flexible transparent tubing about one inch in diameter and about three feet long at the plumbing supplies department of your hardware store. Put a couple of marbles inside the tube and glue corks securely in both ends of the tube. Children can see what happens to the marbles when they lift one end or the other or the middle.

Bubble in a Tube

Using about 3 feet of flexible plastic tubing (see above), securely glue a cork into one end. Fill the tube with water you have colored with food coloring, leaving about one inch of air for a bubble. Glue a second cork into the other end. The child will enjoy watching the bubble travel up and down the tube when the ends are lifted.

Marble in Oil in a Tube

Fill the flexible plastic tubing (see above) with mineral oil or vegetable oil. Put a marble or two in the tube. Glue corks into both ends. The oil will slow the progress of the marble.

Oil Bubble in a Tube

Glue a cork in one end of about 2 feet of transparent plastic tubing. Fill it with clear water to within one inch of the end. Then pour in about one inch of colored lamp oil. Glue in the second cork. The colored oil will always rise to the top when different ends are lifted.

Oil and Water Bottle

Find a sturdy transparent bottle such as a baby shampoo bottle and soak off the labels. Fill it about 1/3 full with water to which you have added some food coloring. Then fill the rest of the bottle almost to the top with mineral oil or baby oil. (Any kind of oil works — these are suggested only because they are colorless.) Glue the top on securely with quick bonding glue. Wiggling or shaking this bottle produces beautiful waves and slowly floating colored bubbles. A simple hand action produces a very pretty effect. This activity tends to be soothing as well.

Roly-Poly Toys

Fill a large plastic panty hose egg bottom with plaster of Paris. Glue the halves together and decorate the egg in any number of ways—perhaps using a permanent marker to draw a face. When tipped it will right itself.

A classical "folk art toy", this appeals to the younger toddlers and infants who are not yet walking. You could put a jingle bell inside for a sound effect . . . just be sure the egg is glued securely shut.

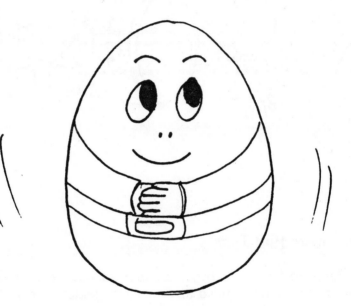

Rolling Noisy Barrel

Find a round cardboard box or barrel such as a bulk ice cream container with a top, the kind of barrel that bulk laundry detergent comes in, or for a smaller version, a potato chips can, coffee can or cornmeal box. Put noisy junk inside such as jingle bells, jar lids, etc. Tape both ends on securely. Glue magazine pictures of objects the child will recognize on the outside of the barrel. Cover the whole thing with clear contact paper to protect the pictures. Let the child have fun rolling this noisy thing around the room.

Homemade Pull Toys

Sometimes people buy pull toys to encourage toddlers to walk. Toddlers don't need any "encouragement" to walk! However, a toddler will enjoy a good pull toy for the cause and effect response the toy gives. That's why commercial pull toys almost always make noise when the child pulls it.

You can make your own versions. A short string tied to any variety of "junk objects" will give children something fun to drag that makes noise when it moves. Keep safety in mind — no sharp edges, nothing small enough to swallow. (Never use as a crib toy.)

Some possible things to use: jingle bells inside a metal can with the top glued on, a number of jar lids with a hole punched in the middle (file hole smooth), an aluminum pie tin, or several tied together . . .

Pounding Benches

Most toddlers enjoy playing with a simple pounding bench where they use a little wooden mallet to pound wooden pegs through holes. The toy suppliers listed in the appendix have several varieties. It is a good "cause and effect" toy and also involves some practice in eye-hand coordination.

Hanging Objects

Hang some interesting things from the ceiling with string. Possibilities are foam rubber balls, beach balls, or stuffed animals. Adjust the length of the string so that the objects hang above the level of the child's head but still within reach. Show the child how to hit the object with his hand to make it swing back and forth. You might try hanging several different objects at varying heights.

While the toddler is having fun wih cause and effect he is also developing shoulder and torso muscles and developing balance.

For variety, show the child how to bat at the objects with paper towel tubes.

Safety note: Be careful that the strings aren't low enough to get around the children's necks. Hanging balloons is not a good idea because when they break they are dangerous to have around toddlers. There have been some tragic incidents of young children choking on balloon rubber.

Fun with a Pulley

Rig up a pulley between the floor and the ceiling of the room. It's best to attach a second pulley to the floor end (Venetian blind style) so children won't get it tangled around their necks. Tie a basket to one rope and show the children how to pull the other rope to raise the basket to the ceiling. When they let go, the basket will fall down to the floor again. They can then give a stuffed animal a ride to the ceiling.

Radio Play

An old radio is a wonderful play tool for toddlers. There are several ways the toddlers can practice cause and effect with a radio. They can turn it on and off. They can change the volume. And, of course, they can change the station. Do they learn to stop turning the knob when they get to a station? Do they move their bodies when they hear music? Do they react to speaking voices? As with any electrical appliance, keep a close eye on this. Try to arrange the cord, if there is one, so that it is not where toddlers would walk. Remember to put the safety plug back in your electrical wall outlet when you are through. Better yet, use a battery operated radio.

CHAPTER 2

Playing with Water

You go outside after a rainstorm and before you can make a quick grab your toddler heads straight for the mud puddle. Usually she beats you there!

Turn your back a minute and you will hear splashing noises coming from the toilet. (Hopefully it was flushed!)

Any type of waterplay is an excellent cause and effect activity, and endlessly fascinating to toddlers. Mothers have known this ever since the bathtub was invented. "When all else fails, put them in the tub." Playing with water is as close to a "compulsion" as anything you could think of with toddlers, so you might as well make it legitimate and gear up for it.

The reason water play holds the attention of toddlers so well is because it produces such a wide variety of responses. Some things pop up to the surface when you release them under water. Some things sink to the bottom when you do the same thing. What wonderful noises water makes!

The youngest toddlers will enjoy just splashing the water and watching it dribble off a washcloth. They are enjoying the feel and sound of water. As children get older they will become more and more interested in "doing things" with water. Possibilities are endless—but here are some favorites for starters.

Sponges

What a great invention the sponge is! A package of inexpensive sponges will find many uses around toddlers besides cleaning.

When using sponges with water play, children will discover many entertaining uses. Squeeze them out and they float. You can make them into little rafts and give rides to little wooden people, plastic animals, etc. You can blow them to make them move.

The "mechanics" of sponges will interest toddlers, and allowing them plenty of time to just play is the best way to let them learn. Later you can offer a challenge: "Can you fill this little bowl just using the sponge?"

Washing Rocks

Toddlers really like rocks. Give them small sponges and some rocks and invite them to wash the rocks. They will discover that rocks change color when they are wet, and slowly fade back as they dry. This is a nice activity to do outside on a warm day.

Pouring

A collection of containers of different sizes and shapes and a tub of water are all you need here. Margarine tubs, cut off plastic bleach bottles, plastic milk jugs, film canisters, coffee scoops, spray can tops, plastic bottles and jars are all possibilities. A small funnel would be a nice addition. Don't present too many at one time. Two or three containers is enough at first. Later you can ask, "What things would you like to pour with today," and allow the child to choose. Pouring is a good way to develop eye-hand coordination.

Dribbles

Poke holes in the bottom of a margarine tub and children will enjoy filling it with water, lifting it, and watching the water dribble out.

Basting

A large meat baster will attract the concentration of toddlers. When you first introduce this to the child it is a good idea to have two—one for yourself and one for the child. "Look what I can do with mine. I squeeze this and bubbles come out. Then the water goes in. Can you do that with yours? Now when I squeeze it I can make the water go in this jar ... watch."

Show the child how to empty one container of water and fill another using the baster.

Plastic Eye Droppers

These, of course, operate from the same principle as meat basters, but on a smaller scale. Instead of using the whole hand to squeeze, the child uses just the forefinger and thumb.

After the child has had a chance to play with it freely for a while, you could have him transfer colored water from one margarine tub to another using an eye dropper. Small molded plastic pet food dishes with two compartments work well for this. A baking pan underneath could catch drips.

Ice Cube Tray Color Transfers

Older two year olds will enjoy transferring colored water in an ice cube tray. Partially fill a white ice cube tray with clear water. Put a few drops of food coloring in one compartment. Put a second color in a second compartment at the other end. The child can transfer the color from one compartment to another using the eye dropper, and will pick up some information about color mixing. If you add a third color — red, blue and yellow — the child will end up with all the colors of the rainbow.

Finally, the child may enjoy dropping these pretty colors onto white paper towels with the eye dropper to make pretty color blotches.

More Eye Dropper Fun

Have children transfer water with an eye dropper from a margarine tub to a dry sponge. "Where did it go?"

They will also enjoy filling small containers such as film canisters, bottle caps, jar lids, etc.

Incidentally, while children play with eye droppers they are also gaining practice using their "pincer" muscles of thumb and forefinger leading toward the coordination skills later needed to hold a pencil and write.

Squeeze Bottles

Save the empty plastic squeeze bottles that dish detergent, and such things as catsup, mustard, glue and shampoo come in. Especially good are the clear plastic bottles. This allows children to see what's going on inside the bottle as well as the squirt.

Children enjoy watching the bubbles come out when they squeeze the bottle under water.

Toddlers enjoy holding bottles upside down and watching the water dribble out. (This is why glueing, using glue in squeeze bottles is an unsatisfactory activity for toddlers. They are most fascinated with watching the glue dribble out of the bottle and will greatly frustrate teachers by wasting large amounts of glue.)

Once the toddler has had plenty of time to play with a squeeze bottle, challenge her to fill another plastic bottle with a small opening.

Washing Things

Very popular activities, all of these. To the fascination of water play you're adding a new interest of toddlers — dramatic play — acting like a grown-up. When water play merges into dramatic play it takes on another dimension. The combination can't be beat to hold their interest.

Wash Dolls

When you give a toddler a doll to bathe, have clothes on the doll and see if the toddler will think to take them off. (Children will usually be able to undress a doll long before they can dress it.) The more real "props" you can provide, the better. A small bar of soap, a washcloth and towel, a comb will do the trick. It might be fun to put a tape recorder nearby and record what the child says to the doll.

Wash Doll Clothes — or Real Clothes

Provide soapy water — and perhaps some rinse water. Show the child how to wring out wet things. It will add extra fun for two year olds if you can rig up a low clothesline and add some clothespins.

Wash Dishes

A real dish drainer, dish tub, plastic dishes, dish rag and warm soapy water will get amazingly accurate imitations from your toddler.

Wash the Car

Outside on a warm day toddlers will enjoy washing their riding toys or small cars and trucks, or helping someone wash a real car.

Bubbles!
Blow Bubbles Through a Straw

Once they get the hang of it, two year olds love to blow through a straw into a bowl of soapy water to make a frothy mass of bubbles. What a delightful effect for their efforts! A great sound too! Let children practice on plain, non-soapy water first to learn how to blow out rather than suck in.

If children suck in and swallow the soapy water, a little won't hurt them, but enough will give them digestive upset. Therefore, supervise closely. Of course, each child will have his own straw.

Bubble Prints

Add food coloring to the soapy water in a margarine tub. When children have produced a froth of bubbles, lay a white piece of paper over the top. When you lift it off a "print" of the bubbles will remain.

Chasing Bubbles

You don't need to purchase commercial bubble soap. Just mix about two tablespoons of dishwashing liquid to a cup of water. A loop made from a pipe cleaner, scissors finger holes, etc. make fine bubble blowers. Your toddler will love chasing after and catching the bubbles you blow, or watching them float away in the breeze outside. Each breath brings a surprise! Try waving a strawberry basket or cherry tomato basket dipped in bubble soap and see what happens!

It's wonderful fun to plug in an electric fan and blow bubbles in front of it. The fan will blow the bubbles all over the room, to the delight of the children. You will, of course, supervise this closely, not letting children put their fingers near the fan. Put the fan away as soon as you are finished with the activity.

Running Water

Faucets and drinking fountains fascinate toddlers because they get the added cause and effect action of turning them on and off. And you can do so much with the running stream of water that comes out of a garden hose! Give a two year old a garden hose to fill a wading pool and she'll be occupied for a long time — and the pool will not necessarily become full.

If you're adventurous and don't mind getting wet on a hot day, show your two year old how to work the nozzle on a garden hose!

Some Typical Problems With Water Play

1. Children get wet. If a child is in the bath tub, of course, this is no problem. But in a child care situation it's a different story.

Waterproof smocks are available from child care equipment suppliers and are a good idea. They cost about $5 or $6. (See appendix.)

The constant reminder, "Keep the water in the tub (or water table)," will help somewhat. Show the child how to hold the containers over the center of the table. Stay fairly close by to calm children down if play starts to get too exuberant. "This water is for pouring, not for splashing." Notice when they're doing it right: "You're doing a real good job keeping the water in the water table today!"

2. The floor can get wet and slippery.

Again, the reminder, "Keep the water in the water table (or dish tub)", will help. Place the water table over a tiled area of the room. You might even choose to protect the floor with an old shower curtain or large, heavy piece of vinyl or vinyl floor runners.

If you cut down the handle of either a string mop or sponge mop, children will greatly enjoy helping mop up.

The above two problems make water play an ideal outdoor activity in warm weather.

Another way to catch drips is to put dish tubs inside a small child's wading pool on a low table or on the floor. Spills land in the wading pool rather than on the floor.

3. Children will often drink the water or suck on bottles or basters.

It's inevitable that children will taste the water. This is one reason why it's important to use clean water each time. Do not let water sit over night. Showing them what to do with materials will help alleviate this. When they know other interesting things to

do with bottles and basters they will be less likely just to suck on them. Supervise.

4. Children sometimes squirt each other with bottles or basters. Say, "These bottles aren't for squirting people — they're for filling and emptying and squirting into these things." If the child persists, get him involved in something else.

5. A common error is to have too many things for the child to play with. You have to leave room for the water! If you have too many toys the child will be too easily distracted and will not be able to play constructively. Better to offer a few well-chosen items and store the rest. Vary them from day to day.

6. It must be noted that children in bathtubs at home need constant close supervision. It is possible for a child to drown in one inch of water. Make sure you have a non-skid surface or decals on the floor of your tub. A child may also be scalded by turning on the hot water. Do not leave the toddler under the supervision of a slightly older sibling.

CHAPTER 3

Banging, Twanging, Shaking

Hand a toddler any new object and he or she will go through a series of test procedures. First it will go to the mouth to see how it tastes. Then the child will probably turn it all around to examine all sides. Then, almost for sure, the child will shake it up and down and bang it against a surface to see what kind of noise it makes.

Cup banging, banging dishes on the table or toys on the window are not only destructive, they can drive a teacher or a parent crazy!

Since toddlers love to make things produce noises, it's a good idea to have a variety of noise makers and to make them available at a time when noise is acceptable.

You can, of course, buy rhythm instruments from equipment suppliers, but there are plenty of instruments that are easy and inexpensive to make, and are a big hit with toddlers. Here are a few samples.

Shakers

Toddlers will enjoy a wide variety of shakers. The primary pleasure in shakers is cause and effect. "I move my hand in this way and it makes a neat noise."

Make a collection of all different types of cans with plastic lids: Film canisters, potato chip cans, pop corn and nut cans, juice cans and coffee cans.

Fill the cans with such things as salt, marbles, rice, beans, nuts and bolts, styrofoam squiggles. Glue the lids on well and decorate if you wish. Tape, and keep in good repair.

If you make pairs of shakers filled with the same thing, older toddlers will enjoy finding the matching can.

Make a "shaker collection" and keep it in a box. "Look. I have all kinds of things in this box that make a noise when you shake them! Which one would you like to try first?" "Shake, shake, shake." "Oh, that makes a loud noise."

Another variation is to use the small plastic Easter eggs, fill them with various substances to shake and glue them shut. These can be stored in an egg carton. Perhaps you can find two eggs each of six different colors and make those match sounds. Then the child will have the color clue as well as the sound clue to find matching pairs. This will also appeal to toddlers' compulsion of fitting objects into spaces when they replace the eggs into the egg carton.

Two aluminum pie tins could be stapled together with objects inside. Test frequently to make sure it's secure and the material inside cannot fall out.

Washboard

A metal washboard (you can still get them in hardware stores) is fun to scrape with a wooden rod.

Multi-Cans Drum

Tape together a number of empty cans of various sizes so they form a circle. Electrical tape or cloth tape works well. Remove the bottoms of the cans and file the sharp edges smooth or cover them with tape or contact paper. Let the child bang on the various cans with a short stick and see what different sounds they make. An unsharpened pencil with a large rubber eraser glued on makes a good drum stick.

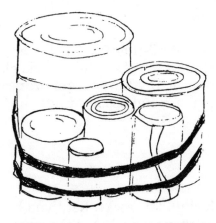

Twanger

An old fashioned door stop that sticks out of the wall makes a wonderful twanging noise when a child snaps it. You could attach one (or several) to a board, small wooden box or the back of a shelf or room divider. Can the children imitate the noise it makes? Glue the ends on securely.

Sand Paper Blocks

Glue sandpaper to one side of a small piece of wood or heavy cardboard measuring about 3" by 4". Attach a knob on the back for a handle or staple a strap or piece of elastic to form a loop on the back. Show the toddler how to slide these back and forth against each other to make a "brushing" sound.

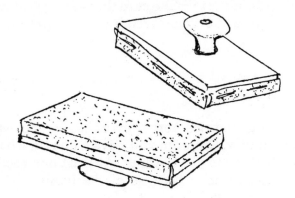

Pots and Pans

Don't forget the all-time favorite kitchen pots and pans band. This can be the most fun of all. Join in and play with cookie sheet gongs, wooden spoon rhythm sticks or drumsticks, pot drums, pot lid cymbals, and a metal spoon "ding-a-linging" inside a metal can.

Rock Band

Give each child two rocks. Let them bang them together to see what sound they make. When the whole group does this you are creating "music" of a unique sort.

Rhythm Sticks

Rhythm sticks or "claves" cost about $1.50 per pair commercially. You can made them from two 9" dowels you can buy at a hardware store or lumber yard. Try different thicknesses. Hardwood produces a better tone. Cut up a broomstick or mop handle.

Wood Blocks

As for sandpaper blocks described above, cut two small pieces of wood about 3" by 4" and attach a small knob on the back of each. Sand the wood smooth to make sure there are no splinters. These also cost about $1.50 commercially. Let children clap them together.

Drums

Drums range in price from a few dollars on up depending on the size and quality. Children will have a fine time banging on a coffee can which costs you nothing. At least one good drum is a very nice thing to have because of the quality of the sound. Tambourines are also loved by toddlers.

Homemade Can Bell

For this you need a can with one end removed, an empty thread spool, string, two buttons, glue, a hammer and a sharp implement like a screw driver. Using the hammer and sharp implement, punch a hole in the end of the can. Remove paper from the can. Tie one button to the end of the string, threading the string through the hole in the button. Tie a knot and thread on the second button so the first button will hang above the bottom of the can. (See illustration.) Thread the string through the hole in the can. Put glue on the top of the can. Thread the string through the spool and tie securely around the top so that the spool is pushed tightly against the top of the can in the glue. Allow the glue to dry. Although the directions sound complex, these are easy to make. Just study the illustration. These make very pleasant clinking sounds that vary with different types of cans. Note: you cannot decorate these with paper or contact paper because it will deaden the sound.

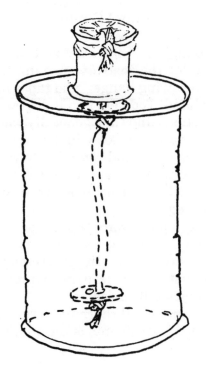

Bells

It would be fun to develop a collection of bells for toddlers to try. Counter bells—the kind you bang on in stores to get the attention of the clerk—are loved by toddlers. There are various jingle bell instruments available commercially which cost between $1.50 and $5.00. You could also securely sew jingle bells onto loops of elastic that can be slipped over the child's wrist.

Bring in an old alarm clock and show a child how to pull the lever to make it ring and push it to stop the ringing.

Bicycle bells and cow bells and bicycle horns are other possibilities. Different hand actions are required to produce these fun sounds. Collect other kinds of non-breakable bells for children to play with. Each will produce its own unique sound.

Instruments I Do Not Recommend for Toddlers

Triangles, Cymbals, Hanging "Gongs"

Triangles and hanging gongs are too difficult for toddlers because you have to let the instrument hang freely with one hand, holding only the string hanger, and tap it lightly with the stick with the other hand. Toddlers find it difficult to coordinate two different hand actions and they generally want to grasp the metal part of the triangle and strike with that as well as the stick.

In order for cymbals to sound right you have to strike them lightly together and bring them apart immediately to let them vibrate. This is too complex for most toddlers. A couple of pot lids will be just as satisfying.

The little metal xylophones are popular best selling toys for toddlers, but children rarely use them for more than random banging and pay little attention to the progression of low to high notes. This type of instrument is more appropriate for older children who like to pick out melodies.

Should you buy commercial rhythm instruments? The main advantage of purchased instruments is the quality of the sound.

The hardwood used for the rhythm claves, for instance, produces a sound more appealing to adults. It is my personal opinion that toddlers' interest stems primarily from the "cause and effect" response rather than the aesthetics of the sound. If the budget is tight, I advise spending your money on other things . . . with perhaps, the exception of one good drum.

Some Things to Do with Instruments

With young toddlers you'll have to allow a great deal of time just to "free play" with the instruments. Don't have high expectations for structured performing.

Start with the Body as the First Rhythm Instrument

"Let's see what sounds we can make just using our bodies." Lead the group in all the variations of clapping you can think of. Clap with flat hands, cupped hands, just fingertips, the back of your hands, etc. Then try patting cheeks. What happens when you open your mouth and pat your cheeks? Pat the top of your head, your knees, the floor. Clap your knees. Rub flat hands together. What else can you think of? "Does it make a noise when we blink our eyes?" "How softly can you clap?" "How loudly can you clap?" "Can you clap slowly, like this?" "Can you clap real fast?" (Later try all of this with instruments.)

A hint: With toddlers and twos in a group, if at all possible, give them all the same kind of instrument. Otherwise, they're sure to want what their neighbor has.

What Made That Sound?

Gather 3 or 4 different rhythm instruments or noise makers. Get a barrier of some sort to block children's view, such as a large box, piece of cardboard or your flannel board.

1. Show children the instruments. Make a noise with each instrument and tell the children what the instrument is called.
2. Hide the instruments behind the barrier. Play one of them. Let the children guess which instrument was played.
3. Let them test their guess by playing the instrument they chose.

Don't expect toddlers to march to music and play instruments at the same time. It's too difficult to do several things at once. In fact, keeping time to music with instruments or body movements is generally too difficult for toddlers.

CHAPTER 4

Making a Mark

Interest in "making a mark" is probably first noticeable when an infant sitting in a high chair discovers the beautiful and subtle result when he smears his strained peas and squash together on the high chair tray.

It is the cause and effect phenomenon that toddlers enjoy in doing art work — rather than the lofty notions of "creativity" or "esthetics". "I do *this* — move my hand to the side — and *that* happens — there's a colorful streak on the paper."

"Art" activities for toddlers should be kept simple. I've often seen a disappointed or frustrated expression on the face of toddler teachers because they spent far longer setting up the project than the toddlers spent doing it. They may be tempted to "doctor up" the child's creation so he will have something presentable to take home, a practice which is totally unacceptable!

Remember that it's the immediate cause and effect — a very momentary action — that appeals to toddlers. It is common for them to show no interest at all in the final product — or even to recognize or remember it at the end of the day. This does not mean that it is not worth doing! In the beginning the toddler pays very little attention to what she is doing. She may not even look at the paper. But as she gains experience, she notices the effect of actions and tries variations. These are the beginnings of eye-hand coordination needed later to learn to write. It is possible that the spark of aesthetic appreciation may be ignited then, also, but that is not the primary objective.

Finger Painting

Finger painting is the "classical" art activity for toddlers — and a very good place to start. They enjoy it as much for the feel as for the cause and effect designs they make.

Shaving Cream

Many toddlers will not like to get their hands messy with paint, but they will almost invariably love to finger paint with shaving cream. A soft, billowy, good smelling mound of shaving cream is almost irresistible. It has the advantage of being easy to clean up, and leaving everything, including the artists, cleaner and sweeter smelling than before. Make sure to rinse their hands afterwards to avoid skin irritation.

Let children paint right on the table top. You could also give children "cafeteria trays" or cookie sheets to paint on to minimize a mess. For variety you could add a few drops of food coloring to the shaving cream to create pretty pastels.

The one criticism I have heard about painting with shaving cream is that children might rub it in their eyes, so supervision is necessary.

Heated Shaving Cream!

It's a wonderful treat, and very soothing, to fingerpaint with heated shaving cream. To heat the shaving cream you can use one of the small electric appliances designed for that purpose. If you cannot locate one of these, simply place the can in hot water for a few minutes. It works!

Commercial Fingerpaint

Commercial fingerpaint is wonderfully creamy and smells good. It costs about $3 a quart. It's a lovely luxury, but there are many recipes for homemade fingerpaint that work very well.

Homemade Fingerpaint

Here are some simple recipes for fingerpaint. Add food coloring or tempera paint for color:

Cornstarch — Water — Glycerine Fingerpaint

Mix 1/2 cup of cornstarch with 1/4 cup of cold water. Then gradually add 2 cups of hot water, stirring to prevent lumps. Cook over low heat until it begins to boil. Remove from heat and add another 1/2 cup of cold water and 1 tablespoon glycerine. The glycerine makes it slippery and slows up the drying process.

Cornstrach — Gelatin Fingerpaint

Mix 1/2 cup of cornstarch with 3/4 cup of cold water to a smooth paste in a saucepan. Soak 1 envelope of unflavored gelatin in 1/4 cup of water. Pour 2 cups of boiling water into the saucepan with the cornstarch mixture, stirring. Cook over medium heat, stirring, until it comes to a boil and is clear. Remove from heat and stir in gelatin.

Starch, Soap and Baby Powder Fingerpaint

Simply mix liquid laundry starch, soap flakes or powder and baby powder to a smooth consistency.

Change Textures

None of the above recipes are sacred. Fool around with them or make up your own recipes. Try adding textures to the paint by mixing in such things as coffee grounds, cornmeal, sawdust or vaseline to vary the experience. Some people like to add fragrance with oil of wintergreen, perfume or cooking extracts. This certainly is pleasant, but it may make children even more prone to eating the paint. Make your own judgement.

The preceding recipes may be used directly on the table top or on trays as suggested for shaving cream. If you want to save the painting, there are two good ways:

1. Make a monoprint. Use any type of paper — inexpensive news-print works fine. Press it over the child's painting on the table top and lift off carefully to reveal a print.

2. Paint on paper. You can buy special fingerpainting paper from school suppliers. It is glossy on one side which keeps the paint from penetrating the paper. You are supposed to wet the whole paper first so it won't buckle. Fingerpaint paper is quite expensive — about $3.75 per 100 sheets. Shelf paper that is glossy on one side could also be used. It's not as good because it is not as sturdy, but it's less expensive. Toddlers have so little interest in their final product, it's really not worth it to spend a lot.

Window Painting

Toddlers love to fingerpaint on a low window. When the paint dries they can use their fingers or a cotton tipped swab to scribble designs through the paint. Mix detergent or powdered window cleaner with the paint so it will wash off easily.

Mirror Painting

What fun to fingerpaint on a mirror and slowly cover up your image! Later the paint can be rubbed off little by little to reveal the image again. "Peek-a-boo!"

Do a Group Fingerpainting

Tape a long piece of shelf paper to a table top and let several children paint at once. They'll enjoy the social aspect.

To introduce fingerpainting, simply sit down and do it yourself, describing what you are doing. Have the child ready to go at the same time so he can join right in. Don't draw anything—just mess around. "Oh look—there's a big blob of blue paint in front of me. I'm smearing it around and around. It feels good. Ooooh, pretty! Can you do that too?"

A technique I've sometimes seen teachers use which I do not recommend is to put your hands over the toddler's and guide their hands. Better to let the toddler approach the material on her own terms.

If you are in charge of a group of toddlers, don't attempt to have them all paint at once. Let two or three paint while the others continue to play at something else. Be sure to protect clothing with smocks and roll up sleeves.

If you don't have a sink close by it's a good idea to have a bucket of soapy water and a sponge handy for quick clean ups.

Using Food for Finger Painting

Although it is common to use such things as pudding, whipped cream, or yogurt for finger painting, with the reasoning that it won't hurt toddlers if they taste it, I do not recommend this practice. I'm of the opinion that toddlers should realize that food is food and there to eat. It's hard enough to get them not to smear their spaghetti sauce! If you use non-toxic, safe ingredients, children will not be harmed by fingerpaint.

Scribbling

Most toddlers really love to scribble. As any parent knows, if you don't watch closely, there will soon be crayon marks on the walls and furniture. Instead, give toddlers plenty of legitimate opportunities to scribble on paper. If you vary the material you give them for scribbling they will learn about different textures and colors. You may even notice differences in their scribbling style with different materials.

Crayons

"Fat" crayons are good to use because they are easy to grip and they don't break easily. It's a good idea to peel the paper off the crayons so the side can be used to make marks as well. The toddlers might enjoy helping you peel the crayons.

"Chunky" crayons are available commercially. They are shaped like hockey pucks and children grasp them with their whole hand. With these crayons children can use large sweeping arm movements on a large scribbling surface such as a piece of butcher paper taped to the floor.

You can make these big crayons yourself. It's quite a bit of work though. Do not do it with children around because the melting wax can be dangerous.

1. Peel the paper off old, broken crayons. (Children can do this part for you ahead of time.)
2. Sort by color.
3. Melt in a small saucepan placed in water in an electric frying pan. (Use an old pan you do not intend to use for anything else again.) It is important to melt the crayons in a pan surrounded by water because crayon wax is very flammable.
4. Pour melted wax into muffin tins you've sprayed with non-stick coating. Let cool and harden.

Marking Pens

The advantage of felt tipped marking pens is that with very little pressure the child gets brilliant streaks of color. Make sure you get *water soluble* markers, not "permanent" markers.

The disadvantages of markers are:

1. Unlike crayons, the amount of pressure a child exerts does not affect the quality of the mark.
2. Unlike crayons, children soon learn that markers color skin very well. Even water-soluble markers can be hard to wash off.
3. Some toddlers like to suck on the end like a bottle, resulting in colored lips and teeth ... therefore, keep an eye on the activity.
4. The caps can be dangerous—just the right size for a toddler to choke on. If the caps get lost the pens dry out and are useless.

Here's an idea to combat this last problem. Mix up some plaster of paris and pour it into an old baking pan. It should be the consistency of very thick cream when you pour it. (Don't pour excess down the drain ... it will clog your pipes forever!) Sink the marking pen tops, open side up, into the plaster halfway up to the open end. Let the plaster harden. Then put the marking pens into the caps like birthday candles. Since toddlers love to stick things in holes, you won't have any trouble getting them to put the markers away.

Chalk

With chalk children experience yet another texture. Colored construction paper is a good surface to scribble on. Try wetting the chalk, letting the child dip it in water.

Chalkboards are fun for toddlers when they learn to make marks disappear with an eraser.

Scribble Decor

Tape a large sheet of butcher paper to a table top and make that known as your scribble table. It can stay on the table several days, even a week or two. Put different things on the table for toddlers to scribble with freely. When the paper gets all filled up, simply remove it and replace it with a clean sheet. This could become a permanent fixture in your room.

One teacher I know uses this paper to cover all kinds of boxes and storage containers in her room. She also uses it for shelf paper, wrapping paper, stationery for notes to parents, bulletin board cut-out letters or backgrounds and even frames for toddler paintings. Her room has a unified decor that really reflects its inhabitants.

Another teacher tapes the butcher paper to the wall for the same purpose. She had been having problems with children coloring on the walls when her back was turned, but when she provided a legitimate place to color on the wall, the problem was resolved.

A Scribble Easel

Tape a large piece of paper to an easel. Tie a piece of yarn about 2 feet long around a fat crayon with a notch in it so the yarn doesn't slip off. Tie the other end to the top of the easel. This is now a "scribble place" where a child may make a mark whenever she pleases, without waiting for an adult to set out the materials. You could attach several different colors of crayons.

Paint in Roll-On Deodorant Bottles

By pressing your thumb hard against the plastic collar and prying underneath with something metal you can pop the ball and collar off roll-on deodorant bottles. Wash out the inside and fill it with liquid tempera paint. Snap the ball and collar back on. You've just made a "giant ball point pen" that's a very effective scribbling tool for toddlers. Bright swatches of paint appear on the paper with minimal mess.

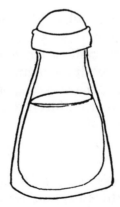

Other Materials

Let toddlers scribble with pencils, ball point pens, colored pencils, and other drawing materials from time to time. Variety keeps it interesting.

What Do You Say?

Don't try to direct or control a toddler's scribbling in any way other than an occasional reminder to keep the marks on the paper. You will notice that a child's scribbling usually follows a predictable progression.

The youngest child usually starts with a series of horizontal lines. Later vertical lines appear. Then, round and round, non-ending circles. Later you may notice a completed, closed circle. Almost all children make "spider" or "sun" patterns eventually with lines radiating out from a central circle. This does not usually appear until a child is well past three.

If you feel you must comment on a child's scribbling, you can say something like, "Wow . . . you made lots and lots of blue marks! They go round and round and round." Don't ask the child what it is supposed to be. At this age they honestly don't have anything in mind. They enjoy making marks for their own sake. Purists!

Paper

It really doesn't matter what kind of paper you use. Even newspaper is fine — children don't seem to mind the print at all. Recycled computer paper, shelf paper, newsprint, paper grocery bags and butcher paper are all inexpensive or free and serve the purpose well. Try also cardboard boxes, egg cartons, wax paper, aluminum foil and rocks for children to paint on.

Brush Painting

Brush painting is messy and requires close supervision, but is very enjoyable to older toddlers and two year olds and worth the effort.

To minimize the mess:

1. Protect children's clothing with smocks. Be sure to roll up sleeves.
2. Protect the floor with newspapers, a large piece of vinyl, or perhaps an old shower curtain.
3. If you're using an easel you may want to cover it with aluminum foil, newspaper or contact paper. (I personally have never minded the sight of an easel with paint drips on it ... I'm glad it's used, and I think it's beautiful ... but other people seem to have a bias against a messy easel.
4. To keep paint jars from tipping over, pour small amounts of paint (1/2″ or so) in baby food jars. Cut holes in sponges exactly the same size as the baby food jar and sink the jar into the hole. The sponge will catch the drips, greatly reducing the mess.

Another idea: Make sure paint cups, (cans or whatever) can't tip over by taping them to the easel tray or putting them in a quart milk carton you have cut in half lengthwise, and taping *that* down.

What Kind of Paint to Use:

Water

Plain water is a good way to start. Toddlers seem to enjoy it as much as paint. They learn how brushes work and you can attempt to show them how to wipe the brush on the side of the jar.

Painting the sidewalk or the outside of the building on a hot sunny day with water is an activity toddlers love. It's fun to see the surface get dark where it is wet and slowly fade as it dries.

Liquid Tempera

This can be purchased in little bottles (poster paints) but is quite expensive in that form.

School supply stores and catalogues sell liquid tempera by the pint, quart or gallon. It's mixed just right and is a good consistency. It costs about $5 a quart.

Powdered Tempera

Powdered tempera is less expensive than liquid tempera, (a 1 lb jar costs about $2) but it can be a bother to mix. The water does not absorb right away. Mix two parts water with one part powdered paint in a jar. Don't shake it, just allow it to sit, and the water will gradually absorb into the paint. When it is all absorbed, stir it a bit with a stick. Prepare the day before you plan to use it.

Try mixing paint in varying thicknesses. Many people use liquid starch as a paint extender. Make the paint thick and gloppy one day, thin and runny another time. Vary the texture and color of the paint. Offer different colors from time to time. Mix things in with paint such as soapflakes, salt, coffee grounds, talcum powder, for a different effect.

Brushes

Standard long-handled "easel brushes" are too hard for toddlers to manipulate. Often you end up with paint dripping down the elbow and drops of paint flung all over the place.

Buy some ½" brushes with 6" handles at the hardware store. These are used for paint trimming. Put one brush in each jar of paint you offer the toddler. Toddlers seem to be able to handle this size of brush quite well.

Brush Variations:

Try these for variety:

— small pieces of sponge clipped on the end of a spring-type clothespin.

— sponges without handles
— cotton-tipped swabs
— feathers
— old toothbrushes
— combs

Easels

Commercial easels from school supply companies cost about $60.

The advantage of an easel is that it presents the painting surface vertically — the child can see the whole thing easily and his arm does not smear across the paint. Although they're nice to have, it is certainly not necessary to have an easel for a child to enjoy painting. If you do use an easel, make sure it is not too high. The paper should be at the child's eye level.

Home made table top easel:

Make a simple cardboard easel by removing one side of a cardboard grocery carton and taping the remaining open edges together so that it forms a triangular tube. This can be taped to the table at the back so it does not slide away when the child exerts pressure with the brush. Tape the paper to the front or hold it in place with clamps or spring type clothespins attached to the sides.

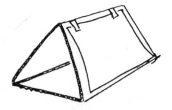

Attach paper directly to a protected wall

Open out a large cardboard box such as a washing machine shipping carton. (You can usually get these from appliance stores.) Nail or tape this to the wall. You can then tape painting paper directly to the wall. You need a little table close-by to put the paint cups on. You could protect the wall in other ways, such as hanging vinyl over the wall or putting contact paper over the wall. Contact paper wipes off easily — but it will pull off paint and damage wallpaper when you remove it. Attach paper to a fence outside. Paint on mirrors or windows (see page 33).

The paint paper does not *need* to be vertical. Toddlers will also enjoy painting on a horizontal table top.

Salt Dribbles

Mix equal parts of flour, salt and water and add liquid paint for color. Pour into plastic squeeze bottles. Then let children squeeze this out in dribbles onto pieces of cardboard. Put the cardboard up to dry for a day if you want to preserve the product for parents. Offer several colors. Toddlers love to use squeeze bottles for anything—here it's legitimate! The colors pool together without mixing, making interesting patterns, and toddlers love to watch the mixture come out of the bottle. Squeezing the bottles gives their hand muscles some practice and strength building exercise.

Sand Painting

Allow the child to dribble glue onto paper from a squeeze bottle, or brush it on from a small amount you have poured in a small container. Sand can be colored by "washing" it with food coloring and letting the water evaporate. Some teachers just mix sand with powdered tempera paint. Then put the colored sand in spice bottles with shaker tops. Let the child shake colored sand or some other granular or powdery substance on the glue. Other types of material to shake onto glue or paste: colored salt, sugar sprinkles, cornmeal, baby powder. (Do not use glitter, because it can cause damage if children rub it in their eyes.) The excess can be shaken off.

Or, allow the child to "fingerpaint" with paste, and then shake the dry granular material over it.

There are a few problems with this type of project. The main one is that most teachers are too limiting. Glue is too expensive to allow the child to use it freely. Often teachers do the sand shaking, putting the toddler into the role of a passive observer. It is a two-step project and the effect is not immediate.

Pasting

Pasting can be an enjoyable experience for toddlers if you are not too concerned with an acceptable looking final product. You might start by letting the toddler tear colored paper scraps into small pieces.

Often young children are most interested in fingerpainting with the paste. Some may not enjoy the sticky feeling on their fingers, and others will be fascinated by it, spending most of the time looking at their fingers sticking to each other, and seeing how paper scraps stick to their finger tips. If they do get a scrap of paper to the page, they then bang on it with their hand to make it stick and sometimes they get frustrated when the paper scrap sticks to their hand instead of the paper.

Sometimes teachers give children pictures or cut up greeting cards to paste and are frustrated when children put the paste on the front of the picture rather than on the back.

Pasting is really a fairly complex process. If you approach it as a good "messing around" experience and generally leave the children alone, it will have value. It loses value when the teacher takes over and does part or most of the project.

Some teachers have had limited success in giving children small cups of glue and craft sticks or cotton tipped swab applicators.

If the adult puts the glue on the paper for the child the value of the project is lost.

Tearing Paper

Get several old magazines or newspapers and tell a small group of children, "These are old and we don't need them any more. Let's tear them up." The sound of several people tearing paper at once is fun to hear in itself and toddlers like the sensation of using both their hands in opposition to each other. Later they can paste their torn pieces to another sheet of paper.

Art Techniques I Do Not Recommend
for Toddlers

1. Most gluing projects. A waste of time for toddlers! (Yes, I realize this is a rash and heretical statement.) The reason is that the act of making something stick on is not a satisfying visible effect — they can't *see* the glue or understand why it happens. So what do they typically do when offered this activity? They dribble the glue, being much more interested in watching the glue come out of the bottle than in what it does on paper. Instead, let them do salt dribbles. (See page 42)

2. Water color trays. Water color trays with the little solid pans of color that you can buy in most variety stores are not good to use with toddlers. The process is too complex. The child must get the brush wet in water, swirl it around on the solid paint to get the color on the brush, make the mark (often the brush is too fragile for a toddler's heavy hand), rinse the brush before starting the process all over for a second color. You end up with a ruined tray of paints. Reserve water color trays for older children.

3. Printing. Potato printing, gadget printing, sponge printing, wonderful projects for children 3 and older, are usually not too satisfying for toddlers. They usually "paint" with the objects rather than printing with them. They move their hand to see the swatch of color — the immediate effect . . . so why not just let them paint?

In all fairness, some teachers of two year olds have, with patience, been able to teach the children to do the printing process successfully. It depends on how much time and patience you want to put into it.

4. Using glitter. Glitter is dangerous to use with young children. If some should stick to the child's hand and she subsequently rubs her eyes it could cause corneal damage.

5. Cutting. Toddlers do not have the coordination in their hands to use scissors effectively. Instead, allow them the pleasure

of tearing paper. To give the child practice in using those muscles of his hand, you could let the child cut coils of playdough with blunt-end scissors. This activity will occupy some toddlers for a long time. Supervise closely ... even though the child will not be successful at cutting paper, hair seems amazingly easy for toddlers to cut!

Some Things to Do with Toddler Art Work

Remember the principle that with toddler art work it's the process, not the final product that is important to the child. For this reason, it's probably okay if you do nothing at all with the art work. Many teachers, however, feel a need to display art work to show parents that it is taking place and parents like to show their child that they value her creative efforts.

1. Many parents of preschoolers have the fanciest refrigerator on the block. The regrigerator is really a good place for children's art work at home. You can attach works easily with magnets and because it's right in the center of things it will give the work importance.

2. Frame it. Find an old picture frame or make one out of burlap or calico or mat board. Then you can change the picture in this frame every few days or so.

3. Paintings can be made into greeting cards. Cut them into rectangles (with the child's permission) and glue these onto the front of a folded white piece of paper to make a card.

4. Paintings and scribbles can also be made into wrapping paper, book covers, box covers, etc.

5. A scrapbook. Of course, you won't want to save every single thing, but it's nice to save representative samples and date them. You'll be amazed at how you can trace a child's development through his or her art work.

6. Use the back of painting or drawings to write a child-dictated letter to grandparents or special friends.

7. Thematic decor. Many teachers like to decorate their room with seasonal or thematic art work done by children. They accomplish this with toddlers by precutting the paper the child is

to paint on into holiday shapes such as pumpkins or bells. If you try to get toddlers to make a particular thing such as a Santa or a flower, you are destined for failure. But when you give children precut shapes on which to paint or scribble, they can paint freely, and gain experience with new types of boundaries. You are gradually increasing their awareness of shapes.

CHAPTER 5

Sensory Exploration

Give a young toddler a new, unfamiliar object and watch what happens. The object will go to the mouth immediately. "How does it taste?" "How does it feel?" "Does it have a smell?" Then the object will be turned over so all sides can be examined. Next she will probably shake it and bang it on the table or the floor to see what kind of sound it makes.

Toddlers vigorously use all of their senses to explore everything. One of the joys of working with children of this age is that the whole world is fresh and new to them. They are busily "gathering data". As they use all of their senses they gather information and gradually absorb concepts such as hot, soft, wet, salty, etc.

Sense of Touch

Patch Work Rug

For next to nothing you can make an attractive rug for the play room. You can obtain out of date carpet samples from a carpet store. Glue these to an old tarp, painter's drop cloth, or other heavy backing material. Some carpet samples come with a fabric binding. These bindings could be sewn to the bindings of the squares next to them. The child will enjoy feeling the different textures as he sits, crawls and plays on this rug.

Play Quilt

This is great for infants as well as younger toddlers. Scraps of variously textured fabric can be sewn together to make a play quilt. Depending on your interest, time and skill with a sewing machine, this can be made quite elaborate by adding various play features. A baby who cannot even sit up yet will enjoy this. Some possible fabrics to use are: satin, velveteen, fake fur, burlap, velour, terry cloth. Some possible "play squares": a squeeker square containing a device that squeeks when pressed (available from craft stores), a pocket with a small stuffed animal attached with a short shoelace to put in and out, a flap that can be lifted, revealing an appliqued picture of a familiar object, a flap attached to velcro that will make a noise when lifted, a zip lock bag with a picture of Mom in it (changeable), a face, horizontal and vertical zippers, a large button with a button hole and a picture under the flap, etc. Of course, these squares could also be sewn together in the form of a book.

Softness

Most homes are full of soft things, but this is not always true of group care environments. It is important to have softness in a toddler's environment ... things that give to the touch. It makes group care less "institutional" and more home-like, and it's pleasing to the senses. The most important soft thing in the room, of course, is a nice, soft adult with a frequently available lap. Other things that qualify are: bean bags and bean bag chairs (make sure seams are securely sewn and stay that way), stuffed animals and soft toys, yarn balls, grass, plants, sand, water, blankets, play dough, carpeting, draperies, pillows ... what else can you think of?

Texture Boards

Glue variously textured materials to a large piece of cardboard for children to feel. Place this where children can reach it. I have seen nicely made texture boards displayed at adult level because the children try to rip things off of it. If kids aren't allowed to touch it, why have it? Usually they can be taught not to tear it apart if a teacher introduces it to a few children at a time and explains what it is for and how to use it, and children see the teacher repair it if it does get damaged.

Possible textured materials to glue on: fake fur, cotton balls, aluminum foil, chamois, foam rubber, netting, sandpaper, velour, burlap, etc.

Texture Box

Glue differently textured materials to all sides of a box.

Texture Cards

Glue textured materials onto heavy cardboard cards. If you make two cards of each texture you can eventually ask a toddler if he can find the card that feels the "same."

Texture Book

Punch holes in heavy cardboard "pages" and put them in a looseleaf binder. Glue a different texture to each page. The stiffness of the pages makes this a better type of book than a cloth book with soft pages. The pages are easier for toddlers to turn.

Texture Snake

Sew variously textured material scraps into a long tube. Use the toe of a sock for the head and sew on features. Stuff it with polyester stuffing material, old nylons, or other stuffing material. A *very* long snake can be a lot of fun to play with. You could use free out-of-date upholstery or drapery samples from a decorating store.

Texture Egg Carton

Glue small patches of different textures in the bottom of egg carton compartments. The child will have to reach in with a pointed finger to feel the texture.

Texture Shelf or Table

Place nicely textured *things* on a shelf or table for children to pick up and feel and carry around. Possibilities: large bones, a chamois, a natural sponge, a large feather (washed), a ball of foil. Change these things frequently. Let children "discover" them and then use the "envelope of language" to talk about the textures with them.

Elephant Feely Box

Cut a hole (about 4" in diameter) in a cardboard box measuring about 14" square and staple the sleeve of an old sweatshirt around it, shoulder end at the hole. Paint an elephant face on the box around the "trunk" and attach felt ears to the side of the box. Put things inside the box from the back and let the child reach in through the trunk and guess what it is that she is feeling. (Of course, a plain box or bag would work too. This just adds an extra element of fun.)

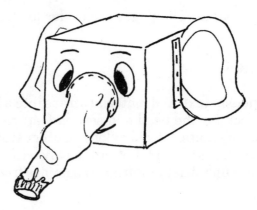

Surprise Bag

It is fun to have a gaudy cloth bag (although any bag or even a sock will do) and call it your "Surprise Bag". (*Surprise* is one of a toddler's favorite words.) Put various things inside the bag and let the child feel the outside of the bag to guess what it is. Then let the child reach in and feel it. Finally let him take out the "surprise".

Choose the Right Objects

As children approach three and have had a lot of experience with the "surprise bag" activity described above, you might try this variation. Put 3 or 4 familiar objects in the bag. Have the child put his hand inside the bag and you name the object for him to identify and take out.

Warm and Cold Stones

Collect some nice, smooth stones—perhaps about ten of them. Put half in the freezer and heat the others in hot water. Then put all the stones on a table. Let children feel the stones and tell you if they're warm or cold. (Rocks retain heat and cold quite a long time.) Some older toddlers may be able to sort them into two piles.

As a variation, do the same thing when you're outside with the child on a hot, sunny day. Let the child feel stones sitting out in the sun and compare them with stones that were buried or in the shade. They could even feel and compare the top side and the under side of a rock, or sunny and shady parts of the sidewalk.

Everyday living gives children many first-hand experiences with the concepts of hot and cold. If you talk about it when opportunities present themselves vocabulary will be strengthened. "Be careful—the soup is hot." "The sun feels warm on my cheeks." "I'm putting ice in the drink to keep it cold."

Texture Ramp

Build a ramp for children to crawl on up to a low platform of some sort. If any height is reached you'll need to have sides on the ramp. The model at the Pacific Oaks College Toddler Yard in Pasadena California has colored Plexiglas in the sides for children to look through. Cover the floor of the ramp with a differently textured material every few feet. Possibilities: Indoor-outdoor carpeting, astroturf, rubber door mat, hemp door mat, woven door mat, wood, formica, etc.

The whole world is made up of textures. Toddlers want to experience all of them. Be conscious of this as children play. A nature walk or even 10 minutes in the yard will offer many textures for the toddler to experience. See if you can let your fingers experience the world of textures the way a toddler's would.

More Warm and Cold Play Ideas:

Using the recipe on page 60 for cooked playdough, let children play with it while it is still warm. Feels good!

Put snow in the water table or dish pan indoors.

Float some ice cubes in the water table or a dish pan.

Fill two zip lock bags with pudding—one with warm pudding, one with cold pudding. Let the child play with these and hold them to her cheeks.

Fill one dish pan with cold water, and one with warm water and let the child play with both, side by side.

Let the children feel the warm air coming from a hair dryer. Direct the air to different parts of the child's body. (Do not leave the hair dryer out for the child to play with.)

Sticky Stuff

Make a Sticky Picture

Cut a large square of contact paper and tape it low on the wall, sticky side out. Put a box of light-weight junk to stick onto it close by. Possibilities: natural materials such as grass cuttings, dried weeds, leaves, feathers, yarn, small fabric pieces, small pieces of paper. The toddler will be fascinated by feeling the sticky surface saying "s-t-i-c-k-y" and pressing things onto it.

Sticky Tape

Is lunch late? Do you need to occupy children for a few minutes while you talk to someone? Just tear off small pieces of masking tape and give them to children. I know one teacher who does this routinely at the busy time after lunch when children are being changed and she is setting out cots for nap time. Children enjoy the stickiness and the magic of the way it stays in place.

Stickers

Most children will do almost anything for a sticker, even if it comes off a banana. You can make your own stickers by cutting patterned contact paper into small pieces and peeling off the backs. They will enjoy sticking these to their skin, peeling them off and sticking them in other places. This fascination is probably one reason why children are so impressed by band-aids. (A box of band-aids is a wonderful birthday present for a pre-schooler. They love the box too!)

Sand Play

Can you remember the pleasure you got from playing in sand as a child? Almost all toddlers enjoy digging. On the purely tactile level, children enjoy the feel of sand sifting through their fingers, and digging down, feeling the coolness of the buried sand contrasted with the warmth of the surface sand. Sand play can be a soothing, calming, absorbing activity for toddlers.

Sandboxes

Sandboxes do not have to be elaborate. The main reason to have boundaries on a "box" is to keep the sand from spreading all over the yard. Railroad ties enclosing a space work well. Large truck or airplane tires, if you can get them are also popular. Get a tarp or plastic table cloth or old shower curtain to cover the sand to protect the sandbox from cats when not in use.

Type of Sand

The sand used for mixing cement—a fairly coarse sand, is good to use in sandboxes. Beach sand is not as good because it is too fine, it doesn't mold well, and it really clings to clothing.

What Type of Toys Do You Need?

The key to a successful sandbox is having interesting things to use there. It seems to be mostly "inexperienced" toddlers who eat sand—they are just exploring the media with *all* their senses. Sit down in the sandbox with the toddler and show him *how* to play in sand. Simply playing there as though you were a child yourself is all you need to do—the toddler will learn by imitation.

A spoon or shovel and a small pail will happily occupy toddlers. Margarine tubs, cut off bleach bottles, spray can tops, coffee scoops and other "good junk" work just as well as purchased sand toys. Don't spend money. A sifter is nice to have. Children will also enjoy poking twigs upright into the sand and drawing lines with sticks.

Plastic or wooden animals and people are also enjoyed. They also love pushing small cars and trucks. Keep these just for the sandbox.

If you can tolerate the mess and the weather is warm, adding a bucket of water will greatly enrich the sand play. Water changes the quality of the sand. It molds easily, tracks and marks stay there. Much spontaneous learning takes place in the sandbox.

Children become aware of the concepts of warm and cool, fine and coarse, dry and damp, empty and full.

You have to "feed the muscles of imagination" in order for it to grow. Playing with mud, sand and water provides sensory input which is stored in the brain's "experience bank" to be used later in life.

When mud forms strange shapes and designs, children notice patterns and make associations. They use the material in new ways to create new effects such as dribbling it in one spot to make a mountain. Children often draw pictures or designs in mud.

Mud lends itself readily to dramatic play. It becomes chocolate cake batter, coffee, pudding, etc. as children pour it into old dishes and pans. This inevitably leads to children acting out the various family roles in a new setting.

Math understandings are absorbed when children measure and pour. "2 of these make 1 of these".

Keeping track of sand toys can be a problem. One solution is to have a "clean up time" at the sandbox before going inside and put all of the toys back into a special container. A covered plastic garbage can attached to a tree, post, or fence works well. Or, use a box or laundry basket and bring it inside each day.

Sand Play Indoors

Sand can be put in the water table, or in dish pans indoors. If you are using dish pans, you can minimize the mess by placing the dish pans inside a child's wading pool on the table. (See page 18). Children will enjoy making roads and pouring almost as much as outside. You can add water to the sand with less mess than if children were sitting in the sand outside.

Having a child-sized broom and dust pan nearby will encourage the child's participation in the clean-up process.

Other pourable substances are sometimes substituted for sand for indoor play, such as rice, cornmeal, birdseed, and oatmeal. Do not use beans because of toddlers' habit of sticking things in their ears and noses. Do not use styrofoam pieces because children "must" chew on these non-edible things, and the small pieces may be inhaled causing a very serious hazard. Sometimes there are cultural or philosophical objections to using food as play materials. I will leave you to make your own judgements on this topic. Probably the most frequent complaint heard about sand from teachers is that children throw it. I have found this usually happens when there are no shovels, pails, scoops or other sand toys to play with. Then, often throwing the sand is the most exciting thing to do with it. Toddlers need a very firm statement from the adult when they throw sand. "Sand is not for throwing. Look, it hurt Jamie's eyes. He's crying. Sand is for digging ... here is a shovel and pail. I will not let you throw sand." Then if the child persists, she must be removed from the sandbox.

Another frequent complaint is that children fill containers with sand, carry it all over the yard and dump it, making a mess of sidewalks and killing grass, or if the sand is inside, making the floor gritty and treacherous. Admittedly, this can be a problem with toddlers and twos. You will need to give constant reminders, "The sand belongs in the box ..." etc. If you can find a small broom or cut down the handle of a larger one and provide a dust pan, children can sweep up their own spills.

Sand Box Cheer

One teacher who is a former cheerleader made up this cheer for children to do after playing in the sand box, before going inside:

"Clap your hands,
Stamp your feet,
Jamie Watson (child's name) can't be beat!

Wipe your knees,
Rest awhile,
Jamie Watson makes me smile!

Clap your hands,
Jump up and down,
Jamie Watson is the best kid in town!"

Play Dough

A toddler program without play dough is almost incomprehensible. It is truly a "basic" play material for toddlers. The primary appeal of play dough, of course, is to the sense of touch. It feels good to squeeze, poke, roll and pound. Toddlers love poking holes in things with their fingers and play dough is perfect for this. Children also gradually absorb concepts of size shape and length as they experience dough. For toddlers, play dough is *not* a creative "art" medium. They are not interested in making things. They are interested in the changes they can make in a substance.

A very real benefit of play dough is that it is a very soothing, calming activity for children and usually holds their attention well. If you need a few minutes to get something done, like preparing for lunch, play dough will do the trick.

Play dough has advantages over several other modeling materials for toddlers.

Modeling clay, or plasticene, is too hard for toddlers to manipulate when it is cold.

Earth clay, or potters clay can be very messy and is sometimes hard to get.

Silly Putty does not keep its shape, is not a great thing for toddlers to taste, and can be hard to get out of hair and clothing.

Purchased play dough costs about $2.50 for a 3-lb can. It's a nice texture, has pretty colors and smells good, but ... why spend the money when it's very easy and inexpensive to make? Try these favorite recipes for homemade play dough for some different textures.

Uncooked Play Dough

Mix together 2 parts flour, 1 part water, 1 part salt. Add a little more flour if it is sticky. Store in a zip lock bag or covered plastic container. Add food coloring to the water for color.

Cooked Play Dough

Materials:
4 cups flour
2 cups salt
4 tablespoons cream of tartar
4 cups water
2 tablespoons oil

Procedure:
Cook over medium heat, stirring constantly until stiff. Let cool and knead. Store in a zip lock bag or plastic container. Add food coloring to water for color. This dough is especially long-lasting.

Salt and Cornstarch Play Dough

Materials:
1 cup cornstarch
1 cup salt
1 cup hot water
1/2 cup cold water

Procedure:
Mix hot water and salt in a pan and bring to a boil. Stir cold water into cornstarch. Add cornstarch mixture to boiling water, and cook over low heat, stirring constantly until it is stiff. Remove from heat and turn out onto a counter to cool. Knead until smooth and pliable.

Baking Soda and Cornstarch Play Dough

Materials:
2 cups baking soda
1 cup cornstarch
1 1/3 cups warm water

Procedure:
Mix baking soda and cornstarch in a pan. Add water and stir until smooth. Bring it to a boil over medium heat. Remove from

heat and pour onto a board to cool. Knead it when it is cool enough and store it in a plastic bag or container. Add food coloring to the water for color.

As with homemade fingerpaint, some people like to add cooking extracts or perfume to give the dough a fragrance. This will make children more likely to taste it.

Play Dough "Enrichments"

1. Warmth. What a special treat to play with homemade dough while it is still warm! Ahhh!
2. Things to poke. Toddlers love making things stand up in the dough like a "birthday cake". Possibilities: popsicle sticks, tongue depressors, large pegs, plastic animals.
3. Pounding hammers. Toddlers sometimes enjoy pounding the dough with the small wooden mallets that typically come with pounding benches.
4. Things to make impressions. All kinds of junk materials are fun for older toddlers to stick in the dough and pull out again to see what kind of mark they make. Large bottle caps, jar lids, forks, a potato masher ... all make interesting marks.
5. Cookie cutters. These are rarely used by toddlers to cut out shapes. Usually they end up being used to pound dough. Sometimes toddlers notice the pattern of the impressions made in the dough. It is hard for the toddler to get the dough flat enough to use cookie cutters for their intended purpose. A rolling pin is difficult for toddlers.

Sense of Taste

Toddlers taste everything whether you want them to or not. They *have* to. Probably the first awareness to develop is to make sure that everything around is *safe* to taste. Once you're beyond that, there are many ways to give toddlers fun experiences tasting new things.

From time to time, not at mealtime, but as a special activity, offer toddlers small amounts of interesting things to taste. Such things as a small slice of raw turnip, a chunk of fresh pineapple, peas just out of the pod, provide opportunities to build vocabulary and talk about how things feel and taste.

Of course, you can introduce new foods at mealtime too.

Cooking Projects

Cooking projects are lots of fun for children. Keep it very simple, and make sure they are all actively involved in the process. Watching an adult cook something will have little value for toddlers and will not hold interest. So let the child do the stirring, pouring, measuring, and chopping (use a plastic knife). Never mind if it's not exact. They will want to taste each individual ingredient as it goes in. Try to think of recipes that are immediately edible, not requiring cooking, baking or refrigerator time. Toddlers may not connect the final product with the process, therefore it's best to do very simple projects with one, two or three children at a time.

Some ideas for starters: Peanut butter and banana sandwiches, fresh orange juice and other fresh fruit juice, fruit salad, lettuce salad, instant pudding, pancakes. Here's a favorite:

Mud Balls

Mix together and form into balls:

Peanut butter
Honey
Dry, powdered milk
Crushed graham crackers
Raisins
Frozen orange juice concentrate

Roll in carob powder or dry instant chocolate drink mix. Other "leftovers" may be added such as: cereal, unsweetened coconut, wheat germ, uncooked oatmeal. A good end-of-the-week project to use whatever is left in the cupboard.

Sense of Sight

A toddler's big expressive eyes take everything in. Toddlers have the full visual capabilities of an adult. If you suspect the child has a vision problem there are simple tests which your pediatrician or community health center can perform. Early detection is extremely important.

Here are some ways to have fun with the sense of sight:

1. Colored cellophane on the window changes the world.
2. Put colored cellophane over the end of toilet paper tubes, securing it with a rubber band. Let the child look through. (The easiest time to find colored cellophane in the stores is around Easter. Craft stores carry it.)
3. Colored Plexiglas is also available and fun to look through. See if you can obtain scraps from a plastics supplier.
4. Put colored water (use food coloring) in baby food jars and look through.
5. You can purchase Plexiglas "color paddles" from toy suppliers for about $3.
6. Look through paper toweling tubing without any cellophane over the end. You see the world in small sections and it looks different.
7. Cut the bottom off a large plastic bleach bottle and wash it out thoroughly. The child will enjoy looking through both ends.
8. Put a gauzy scarf over your head and see what the world looks like.
9. Children also enjoy studying their image in mirrors.
10. Distorted reflections in something like a shiny pot are fun for toddlers. One teacher found a shiny hub cap and has it hanging low where toddlers can see themselves.
11. Show children a 3-way light bulb and switch it back and forth to its different levels of brightness.
12. Put colored cellophane over the ends of flashlights and let children shine these in a darkened room. Flashlights without cellophane are fun too, of course!

Sense of Smell

The world is full of interesting odors and aromas. Toddlers don't seem to mind unpleasant odors as much as adults do. Unlike tasting and feeling and banging and looking at things, toddlers do not consciously go up to something and smell it. But they *do* smell things.

Things to Smell

Collect some items with an interesting and distinct odor such as perfume, cedar shavings, spice bottles, and candles. Simply say, "I have something interesting for you to smell," and put it up to your own nose and smell it. Then put it under the child's nose. The child will quickly get the idea of what "to smell" means.

Smells are so closely associated with tasting that the toddler will immediately want to put the substance in her mouth, so do supervise, and say something like, "This is for smelling, not for tasting."

Go on a Smell Walk

Take a short walk around the building or outside to discover different smells. You might "arrange" some smells ahead of time.

Food Smells

Whenever there is food around you have an opportunity to talk about smells.

A popular game with older children is to blindfold them and let them guess what they are smelling or tasting. Most toddlers are afraid to have a blindfold tied over their eyes, so that kind of guessing game is not appropriate for this age. Older toddlers may cooperate if you say, "Close your eyes and try to guess what this is." Talk about the aromas of food yourself. "Mmmm ... it smells like we're having spaghetti for lunch today."

Sniff Bottles

Wash out plastic squeeze bottles such as mustard and catsup dispensers or dishwashing liquid bottles. Put something with a strong odor inside or saturate a cotton ball with a liquid fragrance. Fasten the tops securely with glue or strong tape. Then show children how to squeeze the bottle to make a puff of air come out to sniff. Possibilities: almond extract, perfume, cloves, vinegar, lemon extract, garlic. Caution: Toddlers will probably try to get the tops off to get at whatever is inside and taste it. Be sure that whatever you use is nontoxic just in case they succeed. (You can expect a toddler to suck on anything that is remotely shaped like a baby bottle.)

Sense of Hearing

"Wow! What a loud truck!" "Listen, do you hear the birds?" "Who is that laughing? It sounds like Susan, doesn't it?" Your "envelope of language" will help a child's awareness of sounds — and auditory discrimination which is ultimately important for language development and later learning to read.

Give a child a new object and he will always test it to see what kind of noise it makes. Toy manufacturers are aware of this. If they can add a "sound consequence" to a toy it will be that much more interesting to the child. Therefore, you have teddy bears that squeek, push toys that rattle and click, cars that beep, etc. (See pages 21–26 for some simple noisemakers you can make.)

Go on a Sound Walk

Give children a small stick like an unsharpened pencil. Let them tap all kinds of things in the room and/or outside to see what kind of sound it makes.

Tape Recorder Fun

Record familiar sounds and see if children can identify them. Possibilities: a car starting, dog barking, vacuum cleaner, dish washer, horn honking, toilet flushing, doorbell, someone knocking on the door, telephone ringing, the Sesame Street theme song, and voices of familiar people.

Hearing Tests

Because of the frequency with which children under three get head colds and ear infections, young children are at high risk for suffering temporary or permanent hearing losses. Naturally, this can have serious effects upon their ability to learn.

If you suspect a child has a hearing loss, check it out with a pediatrician. Many county health departments also conduct free hearing screenings for young children.

Because of the serious negative consequences of hearing losses on the development of a child's intelligence in these early years, it is important to be aware of hearing losses and treat them immediately before permanent damage is done.

CHAPTER 6

Mimicking

In the normal, routine functioning of the "free play" time in the toddler room Timmy gets down on all fours and says, "Meow, meow." The teacher says, "Oh, look, Timmy is pretending to be a kitty. I bet I can be a kitty too." Soon there are numerous kitties crawling around the floor.

Lunch is over and the teacher is wiping the table with a damp rag. Next to her are several children who are also wiping the table with damp rags. The teacher bends over to pick up a piece of food that has fallen on the floor. The children also look for fallen food and pick up crumbs.

A young child at home talks to "daddy" on a toy telephone. Another child "reads" a storybook to his teddy bear.

"Monkey see, monkey do." Mimicking behavior seems to be a basic learning style for primates — and toddlers are the champions for humans. Toddlers are learning that they are separate human beings and are constantly making the discovery, "I can do that too!" "My body will work that way too." "I can make a sound just like that!" Their self-esteem grows as they discover more and more things they can do "just like Mommy" (or Daddy, or Teacher or friends.)

So, if you want to get a toddler to do something, just start doing it yourself. It's very effective teaching strategy.

Follow the Leader Games

Many simple variations of "Follow the Leader" will find success with toddlers. You don't have to announce the game, or appoint a leader or have everybody participate. Just start imitating someone else or start doing something yourself.

— Call attention to a child's unusual actions and start doing it yourself.
— Clap your hands and tap the other parts of your body and children will mimic you. You can name the body parts as you do this.
— Start dancing when you hear music and you'll have a bunch of dancers.
— This is even a way to have children help clean up. Make it look like fun and perhaps accompany yourself with a song: "I'm putting the pegs in box, box, box, and Jamie is helping me too."

The Call and Response Game

A child calls out something: "Da, da, da!" You answer: "Da, da, da!" The child is likely to answer you back: "Da, da, da!" Go back and forth a few times. Then change your response slightly, "Doh, doh, doh," and see if the child changes also. This is the very beginning of communication. You "notice and acknowledge" each other.

Funny Noises

Make funny noises of any type and watch children mimic you. You mimic their noises too. Don't limit yourself to voice noises. Tongue clicking, clapping, tapping hollow cheeks, stomping are other sounds to make and mimic.

Sound Effects

Toddlers often make wonderful sound effects while they are playing. Encourage this form of expression by joining in.

Can You Do What I Do Game

Make your own melody to this chant:
"Can you do what I do, I do, I do. . .?
Can you do what I do, just like me. . .?

Do different actions and watch children imitate you.

Later, when children are very familiar with this game, a child can be the leader. "Can you do what Jenny does, Jenny does, Jenny does. . .? etc. However, if you go from one child to another to have them take turns being the leader, you can expect them all to do the same action the first child did. You might decide this is okay. It's wonderful for the ego to be the leader and have everyone copy you, no matter what you do.

Dramatic Play

Mimicking adult behavior is basic to dramatic play or "pretend play".

A toy telephone is usually one of the first toys we see toddlers use for this purpose. A child as young as 8 months will put a toy phone receiver to his ear and happily babble into it. "Pretending", using one object to symbolize something else, represents the very beginning of abstract thinking in young children.

Do toddlers realize that they will be grown-ups one day? They seem to, as they closely observe adults and imitate them in their play.

Dramatic play toys and "props" need to be simple and quite realistic for toddlers.

Dramatic play can be greatly enhanced in value if an adult or school age child plays with the toddler, giving words and structure to the play. It especially delights toddlers if you occasionally play "the baby".

Some Good Props for Toddler Dramatic Play

A real pot, a wooden spoon, and something to "stir" like large wooden beads will draw the attention of a toddler.

The very basic "playhouse" furniture will be of interest to toddlers. They seem to show an increasing interest in this as they approach two.

A small table and chairs will get much use. The inexpensive plastic parsons' tables available at bargain stores are fine for toddlers. Glue the legs in, or the table will keep falling apart.

Because it is small and light, it will be easy for the toddler to move around. Toy suppliers and stores, of course, have many varieties of small tables for children.

Small, low stools with no backs from an unfinished furniture store provide good, inexpensive seating. Toddlers seem to find them easier to get on and off of than chairs.

Dishes

Instead of buying miniature play dishes which sometimes break easily, I recommend giving toddlers the real thing — some old plastic tableware and pots and pans. Perhaps you can pick some up at a garage sale.

Cans and Boxes

Save empty cans and boxes you use in your own cooking. Clean them and make sure there are no sharp edges. The boxes especially will get damaged as children play with them. Just throw them away and replace them with new ones. The ever-changing variety will keep interest high.

Stove and Sink

Most toddler programs have a child-sized set of kitchen appliances. There are many manufacturers of this type of furniture. Generally, it's worth it to buy the sturdier, more expensive type for group care situations. I have one favorite that has several distinct advantages. It is produced by Learning Products, Inc. and is distributed by numerous suppliers. It is called the "Housekeeping Cube". It has a stove side and a sink side and is built like a cube rather than being rectangular. It is therefore not tippy like most others and climbing toddlers are less likely to be hurt. Made of soft red plastic, it has no doors to pinch little fingers, and no sharp corners.

I have often seen very fine homemade toy appliances. You don't have to be elaborate if you don't want to spend a lot of money. You can paint "burners" on a simple board, add a few knobs and have an adequate substitute stove. A dish tub with a dish drainer next to it will be recognizable as a sink.

Dolls

Sturdy, well-made dolls are best — with arms and legs that will not come off easily because toddlers are not gentle with dolls. I like dolls with rubber bodies so toddlers can bathe them. Try to get a male or "unisex" doll as well as a female doll. Boys like playing with dolls too.

Cloth dolls and stuffed animals have always been loved by toddlers. Stuffed animals can easily be given a male name and balance the preponderance of female dolls. And you can make male cloth dolls.

Doll Bed

Putting a child to bed is something a toddler has certainly watched an adult do and is something they like to imitate in play. Make sure the doll bed is large enough and sturdy enough for a child to get into, for they surely will try, even if the bed is way too small. Lacking a doll bed, you could use a large cardboard box. The bedding is more interesting. A small pillow and a blanket or two will get much action from toddlers. Covering the baby and tucking it in is an interesting activity. Small dish towels make good doll blankets.

High Chair

I do not recommend purchasing a doll high chair unless you can afford a very sturdy one. The toddler is sure to try to climb into it, even if it is obviously too small, and most will break quickly.

I have seen classrooms where the legs of a real wooden high chair have been cut down so the chair sits about 6" off the floor. If garage sales are your "thing" this would be fun to have, because children really enjoy sitting in it and pretending to be fed.

A Mirror

A large unbreakable mirror is a good thing to have. It will find many uses as children develop their self-image. Toy suppliers have polished steel and Plexiglas standing mirrors that sell for about $60. I prefer the Plexiglas because it gives a clear, undistorted reflection. Stay away from mirrors made of foil because they scratch and tear easily.

You can also buy mirrored Plexiglas sheets from plastics suppliers. (Check your Yellow Pages under Plastics.) It costs about $160 for a 4' by 8' sheet. You can cut this with a small hand-held electric saw. A sheet this size would be large enough for several mirrors. Perhaps you could glue a piece of Plexiglas mirror onto the back of a cabinet. Put one at your diaper changing counter too. Use epoxy or other strong-bonding glue.

You could also saw remaining scraps into rounded shapes that children can carry around. Cover the edges with tape.

Dress Up Clothes

Dress up clothes must be easy for toddlers to get on and off. Cut them down so they don't drag on the floor. Front buttons can be replaced with velcro, or enlarge button holes and sew on new, large, colorful buttons. Take a look at your dress up clothes and see what dressing skills you can provide practice for. A simple zipper that does not come apart at the bottom is easy to manipulate, especially if there is a large ring on the zipper tag to grasp. Buckles are very complicated for toddlers. Snaps are extremely difficult, requiring precise positioning and considerable finger pressure from both sides. Tying is out of the question for toddlers.

Hats

Hats are a big hit with toddlers! Gather a big collection of all kinds of hats. You can buy a hat collection from toy suppliers, but you can usually scrounge some for free. Hats are easy to get on and off and what fun to see yourself transformed by a wonderful headdress!

Purses, Etc.

One compulsion of toddlers is to fill and empty containers and carry things around. Purses are perfect for this compulsion. Also collect lunch boxes, a brief case, shopping bags and other such containers with handles. It's a good idea to have a box of "purse junk" available to put in purses. Otherwise, toddlers will find other things such as crayons and puzzle pieces. Old keys, wallets, check books, junk mail, combs, empty lipstick containers, appeal to children because they are used by adults.

Shopping Bag Center

Get a bunch of shopping bags with handles and hang three or four on a peg board. Put small objects in the bags and change them frequently. The objects might include junk mail; clothespins, small toys such as plastic animals, clean rocks, and shells. No object should be small enough for a child to choke on.

Shoes

Ladies' pumps with wide, block heels about 1" high are great fun. Toddlers like to stick their feet in them, shoes and all, and go loudly "clacking" around the room.

Strollers and Carts to Push

Pushing things is a toddler compulsion. A sturdy doll stroller is a good purchase, though expensive. One very popular toy in toddler programs is the small grocery cart children can push around. These can be purchased at variety stores and seem to hold up surprisingly well.

Miscellaneous Enrichments

Props such as dish towels, dish drainers, pot holders, cloth napkins, plastic flowers in an unbreakable vase, a real telephone, magazines, etc. all add realism to toddlers' dramatic play. Putting out different things from time to time will keep novelty and interest high.

Playhouses

A large cardboard box such as one which a washing machine may come in or simply a blanket thrown over a card table will hold much appeal for toddlers because they love crawling into small, dark spaces. (See page 119 (patchwork playhouse) for a thorough description.)

A Window Scene

If you want to add a touch of "hominess" to the decor of your house corner, a window scene is fun. Find a large poster of an outdoor scene, or draw one yourself. Cover with clear contact paper and attach to the wall about 3 feet up from the floor. You could attach a curtain rod to the wall and hang real kitchen curtains. Or, cut curtain shapes out of checkered contact paper and stick this on over the scene.

CHAPTER 7

Language Development

The use of language for communication is said to be one of the things that distinguishes humans from other living things on the planet. Toddlers are becoming more "human" every day as they acquire language at a dizzying speed. The "baby" of one year uttering a few single words (like "mine!" and "no!") will turn three with hundreds, even thousands of words under his belt, putting together short sentences, and will have mastered most grammatical patterns of his native language. With the acquisition of language comes a capacity for more abstract thought.

As you know, toddlers are great imitators. The first thing a young child does is imitate the rhythm and melody and individual sounds of a language without putting together actual words. (Just like you can probably "imitate" Italian, say, without using actual words or knowing the language.) This stage of language development is called the "jargon" stage. As a child plays you will hear him carry on what sounds like a very intelligent conversation totally in nonsense syllables.

When children put together a string of nonsense syllables in their typical babbling, it's not as useless as it might seem. They are giving practice to the muscles which produce the sounds of our language. They are also learning the typical rhythm and intonation patterns of language.

Gradually, more and more words will creep into this jargon. Many two year olds talk to themselves as much as they do to other people. You will notice some wonderful sound effects accompanying their play: "Brring," "whang, whang," Zoom-zoom-zoom," and very often words accompany action.

Twos genuinely enjoy pointing to things and naming them.

There are numerous things you can do to enhance language development. Give children a broad base of experience. Seeing a real cow will have more meaning than looking at a picture and being taught to say, "cow". There's a big difference between verbalization and comprehension. Short trips and providing many things to handle and examine will be very valuable.

Be very conscious of your role as a language model. Eliminate "baby talk" from your speech, even though it sounds cute. Toddlers need "straight talk" in a normal tone of voice and a fairly slow pace. Use full sentences whenever you can. When a child asks, "What's that?" rather than saying, "a record player," respond. "This is a record player." As much as possible use nouns instead of pronouns. Say, "Roll the *ball*" instead of "Roll *it*," "Put *the pegs on the shelf*," rather than "Put *them* over *there*." Be as specific as possible with location words too. "The pegs are on the *bottom* shelf *beside* the puzzles." Contrast the language learning possibilities of the above sentences to a reply where you simply point in the general direction and say, "over there." Also describe children's actions during normal activities of the day, especially using the "-ing" form of the verb. "Cindy is jump*ing* up and down." Be sure to use good pronunciation and grammar. It takes practice and a conscious effort to speak with such clarity. You'll find it does get easier.

Naturally, children make numerous mistakes as they acquire standard speech patterns. Instead of correcting a child directly, simply "reflect" the phrase back to the child as a natural part of your own speech, in its correct form. For instance, if a child says, "Her done it," reply, "Yes, Jason, she did it."

Talking is communicating—having the ideas in one head register in another head. One of the first conversational skills to accomplish with toddlers is to let them know they have communicated. If a child points to the juice pitcher and grunts, instead of just pouring the child some juice you can say, "Oh, I see you want more juice. I will pour you some in your glass." At this point you are translating grunts. Soon you can encourage children to use words rather than grunts, and you can expand on single word utterances. Child: "Crayons!" Teacher: "You want to color with crayons, Joey? Okay, I'll get you a piece of paper and you can sit next to Rachel."

When toddlers verbalize they usually either talk to themselves or to adults. What communicating they do with other children often involves the territorial imperative. "My truck!" When you hear children trying to talk to each other see if you can help.

Looking back on notes taken in a toddler classroom several examples of good talking to children emerged. A child who was just beginning to form sentences said indistinctly, "Come over here." The teacher said, "Jamie, did you hear Robbie? He said he wants you to come over here." The teacher sat on the floor with some photographs of the children. Two children joined her. "Who's this? Why is she wearing a bathing suit?" She also talked directly to one child, an older two year old. "What did you do this morning before you came here, Annie?" An outcry arose from across the room. The teacher asked, "What's the matter?" The child pointed. The teacher said, "You need to tell Robbie. Say, 'That's mine. I'm playing with that now.'" The child repeated those words to the offender and, amazingly, the toy was given back. Another territorial imperative outcry: The teacher said, "Jamie, do you hear what Kimmie is saying? She said, 'Mine!'. She has that chair now. Here's one for you." A child brought over a torn book and held it up to her. The teacher said, "Oh, I see this page is torn. Do you want me to tape it together?" He nodded. "Okay, let's go and get the tape." At snack time she asked, "What kind of juice do you think this is?" Child: "applepine." Teacher: "Oh, pineapple — yes, I think you're right."

What this all boils down to is being "tuned in" to children and aware of their efforts at communication and how to expand on them.

Fingerplays

Two year olds enjoy simple fingerplays (poems accompanied by simple hand movements). Some will only kind of "half" do it but they enjoy involving their hands and body with making sounds. You can make it very simple by having only one cue for them to listen for — such as crouching down and waiting for the word, "Pop!" to jump up in "Pop Goes the Weasel". There are many fingerplay books on the market. (See bibliography)

Chanting

Toddlers do a lot of "chanting" to themselves as they play — often a rhythmic repetition of several syllables. "Do-da-do-da-do-da . . ." If you hear this, try to pick up on it and mimic it along with the child in a playful sing-song way.

You can do this in reverse. Produce your own simple rhythmic chant while you're sitting on the floor playing with a child. Pause and look expectantly at the child and see if she mimics *your* chant. Vary your intonation to a question mode and back to a statement mode. You are teaching the child to play with sounds which will eventually give more flexibility and capability with real words.

"Blurple, purple, blurple, purple, blurple . . ."

Nursery Rhymes

Traditional "Mother Goose" rhymes as well as some more contemporary poetry delight toddlers. These rhymes play with sounds, just the way toddlers do. Don't worry if children don't

understand all of the words. "Hickety-pickety-my black hen. . .",
"Deedle, deedle, dumpling, my son John . . ." "Dance—diddelty-
poppety-pin . . ." These phrases are fun to say and are musical
and rhythmical in effect. *The Puffin Book of Nursery Rhymes*
(Puffin Books) costs $1.95 and has hundreds of rhymes. Chant
these rhymes as you push children on the swing, wait for lunch,
change diapers, clap your hands with a small group of children
and at other odd moments of the day. Try leaving off the last
words of lines of familiar rhymes and see if children will say
them.

Singing

Few toddlers can carry a tune, but they enjoy singing and you
will notice that their voices go up and down in the right places
when they are familiar with the song, and they approximate
rhythms with increasing skill. "Ring Around the Rosie" and
"Twinkle, Twinkle Little Star" are the easiest melodies. Traditional nursery rhyme melodies are a good place to start. Try
chanting the "Ring Around the Rosie" melody singing, "na, na,
na," instead of words. Sometimes the toddler will join in with a
fairly accurate imitation. If you sing a lot, your toddlers will sing
a lot. A musical environment helps generate musical children.

Hollering

Cut the large end off a bleach bottle and wash it out thoroughly. You have a megaphone. (Children will also enjoy looking
through both ends and it may become a hat.)
Did you ever put a bucket over your head and holler? Try it—
it's fun! Toddlers will get a kick out of it too.

"Uh-Oh"

Rather than being a word, this is more of an intonation.
Many languages use this same intonation to notify that something is amiss. Because toddlers spill things and knock things
over so much, they learn this expression very early. Since it
usually generates some action or attention, many toddlers de-

velop an uh-oh-game. Sometimes they say "uh-oh" *before* they dump something. It's a warning ... act fast!

Cardboard Tube "Hummer"

Cut a circle of wax paper about 5" in diameter. Attach this to the end of a cardboard toilet paper tube with a rubber band. Punch a small hole half way up the tube. Show children how to sing into the end of this to make a tickly buzzing sound. Can they sing the "Ring Around the Rosie" melody into it?

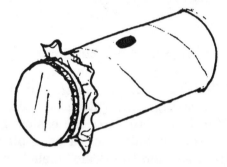

Labelling

Toddlers, true scientists of living, enjoy naming things. One word utterances, "Chair", "Doggy", come before whole sentences. It seems to be with great satisfaction that toddlers will point to objects or pictures and name them ... as if to say, "I know what that is!"

"Receptive   language" — understanding — comes   before "Productive language" — speaking — sometimes long before. Children usually utter at least one or two words by their first birthday, but they differ greatly as to how many words they speak. This, by the way, does not always have a direct relationship to intelligence. Understanding is what counts.

Surrounding children with a lot of meaningful language is very important to development. The "envelope of language provided by adults will give children data upon which to build their own language skills.

There are many simple games and activities to give toddlers experience with words and expand their receptive and productive vocabularies.

The Where Is It? Game

Name things in the room and see if the child can point to them or go over to them. Use real objects. Have a puppet do the asking. Toddlers love to perform for a puppet. "Where is the rocking chair?" Later let the child find objects in pictures on a magazine page or picture book page. At first you will concentrate on nouns ... "things". Later you can ask children to find descriptive adjectives or verbs, actions. "Find something *soft*." "Find something that is *flying*."

Play "I See"

As you're going for a walk outside, say, "I see a tricycle. Do you see A TRICYCLE?" If the child points to it, go on to another item. If not, point to it yourself or go over to it. The child will catch on.

Matching Pictures to Real Objects

Mount drawings or magazine pictures of real objects in the room on large cardboard cards. Cover them with clear contact paper. Hand a card to the child and say, "This is a picture of an orange. Can you find the real orange in the room?" Have the child take the picture over to the real object.

Body Parts

Have a child point to and later name body parts on himself, a doll, an image in a mirror, in pictures or on you. With older toddlers talk about the function of the body part. "Point to what the doggie eats with," "hears with," etc.

The "What's That" Game

You point to an object or a picture of an object, ask "What's that?" and see if the child can name the object. The child must produce the word, not you. Toddlers seem to find great enjoyment in this activity. Once they get the idea that certain combinations of sounds represent particular objects, they seem to be on an endless quest to learn more words and proudly pronounce them. They have entered the "productive" stage of language development.

This is the time when parents usually start collecting cute sayings of toddlers that eventually become part of family lore:

> Jamie thinks a thing you put on your head to keep it warm when you go outside is a "hat-on", (because he has most often heard it: "Put your *hat on.*"

> Zach's family has a dog named "Bodie". His parents often played a game with him. "Zach—where'd bodie go?" Zach sees another dog on the street and excitedly points and says, "Bodiego, bodiego!" (which at this point is his generic term for "dog.")

Picture Books—Purchased and Homemade

When toddlers are in this "labelling" stage of language development, they are usually not ready to listen to stories with continuing plots. They do, however, greatly enjoy sitting on your lap and looking at pictures, pointing to things and naming what they see in a book. You can play both the "Where is it?" and the "What's that?" game as you do this.

Homemade Books

Homemade books for toddlers need to be sturdy and able to withstand wear and tear. It is important to teach children a respect for books from the very beginning and not allow them to tear pages. But toddlers' hand motions are not always going to be gentle so it's best to make pages that will not easily be destroyed.

Stiff pages are easier for toddlers to turn and the hinge action of the pages fascinates them.

Homemade books are such fun to make and provide such enjoyment you'll probably end up with quite a collection before long. Then you can store and rotate them. A book a child hasn't seen in 3 or 4 weeks will seem almost new.

Zip Lock Bag Books

These are fun to make, and very versatile. Simply take several small zip lock bags and sew them together along the bottom edge opposite the zip lock closing. A regular overcast stitch works fine. Now cut some cardboard to just fit inside the bags. (This makes the pages stiff and easier to turn.) Then find magazine pictures or photos to slip on either side of the cardboard.

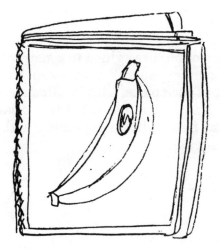

You can change these pictures as often as you like, giving the child frequent variety.

Looseleaf Notebook Picture Book

Purchase a small ring binder. Glue magazine pictures on both sides of a piece of construction paper or thin posterboard. Punch holes with a hole puncher and reinforce the holes with reinforcement rings. Then cover both sides of the pages with clear contact paper. Repunch the holes. Put several pages like this in the binder. You can change the pages as often as you like to keep interest high and emphasize certain concepts. It gives toddlers a very sturdy book which they can carry around and handle freely. Try to find a very small ring binder. Toddlers find this appealing.

Photo Album Book

Put photos and magazine pictures under the magnetic plastic pages of a photo album. Again, these are stiff pages and it is easy to change the pictures. You might make a collection of pictures all of one type of thing, such as dogs or cars. A "baby" book with many pictures of babies is very popular with two year olds who are proud that they are no longer babies.

Sewn Paper Book

Assemble pages of pictures glued to construction paper and covered with clear contact paper. You will want two pictures, side by side on each side of each piece. Vinyl wallpaper samples would make good covers. Put the wallpaper cut to the same size as the paper on the bottom. Sew right up the middle with a large stitch on your sewing machine.

Magazine Picture Books

Women's magazines are some of the best and simplest picture books for toddlers. They are full of pictures of things familiar to young children: kitchens, food, pets, children, and mommies. They will greatly enjoy sitting down and paging through a magazine with you.

Picture File

Every good preschool teacher has a "picture file" — a collection of interesting pictures cut out of magazines. There's no reason why parents couldn't have one too. Teachers often glue the picture to a piece of construction paper and then cover it with transparent contact paper to give it a longer life. You can use the pictures in various ways as children get older, stimulating new levels of language and thought development.

You can elaborate. "Yes, that is a doggy. He looks soft and cuddly, doesn't he? I wonder if he's hungry?"

You can expand the child's understanding of categories by finding many variations of things — many different kinds of birds, for instance. (Of course, children learn best by seeing the real thing, but pictures will reinforce their understandings.)

Children of about two can do simple sorting. Have a collection of two kinds of things — for instance, cars and dogs. Say, "I got these all mixed up. Would you put the pictures of cars over here and the pictures of dogs over there?"

Scrapbook

Develop a scrapbook of photographs and pictures of people and objects familiar to the child. This is a "real life" word book pertinent to that child. This will become a favorite book.

Word Cubes

Use a plastic photo cube as a vocabulary builder. Simply insert magazine pictures or photos of familiar objects on all 6 sides of the cube. The child can turn the cube around and "discover" pictures on new sides. You can change the pictures frequently to provide ongoing "surprises".

Focus Vocabulary

Although children absorb words out of thin air like a sponge at this age, some teachers like to focus on certain vocabulary words each week, "saturating" the environment with the real thing and many pictures. If possible, it's always good to go from the concrete to the abstract. First show them a real cat, then lots of pictures of cats. One teacher "hides" pictures of her "focus vocabulary" words in little nooks and crannies all over the room — on baseboards, on the undersides of tables and chairs, in cubbies, etc. and the toddlers have fun "discovering" them all week.

Flannel Board Progression

The flannel board is a good gimmick to use with toddlers because it holds their attention. They are fascinated by the magic that makes things stick to it. And you have endless variety. Just cut pictures out of magazines, put clear contact paper on the front and felt on the back.

> *Step 1 — Introducing.* You have four or five pictures. Name each one as you put it on the flannel board. "This is a cat." "This is a duck ..."

> *Step 2 — Comprehension.* Have a child point to the object you name. "Which one is the cow?" They could either pick the cow from pictures on the floor and put it on the board for you, or take it off the board and put it in the box for you.

> *Step 3 — Production of Speech.* You ask, "What's this?" If the child names the object you point to correctly she can put it on the board or take it off.

You can certainly buy flannel boards from school supply companies (usually for about $16). They are very easy to make though, and far less expensive to construct yourself. Simply glue a piece of flannel or felt stretched taut over a piece of plywood or heavy cardboard. If you use shelf units for room dividers you could glue felt to the back of one. In a bright color, it will be more attractive than the back of the shelf unit, and you've created a new "learning center". Provide children with a box of felt scraps of various colors and shapes and children will enjoy playing here independently.

Puppet Packs a Bag

Your pet puppet announces that he's going on a trip to spend the weekend at his grandmother's house (or wherever). He brings out a little suitcase, which will in itself be fascinating to the toddler. Then he solicits the toddler's help in finding the items to put in his suitcase. "Bring me the yellow ball." "Now I need a cup." "I have to have a book." "Bring me something soft."

Matching Cards

With these games you are working on the concept of "same and different" as well as building vocabulary.

Buy two of the same issue of a magazine. Women's magazines usually provide the best pictures. Cut out the same pictures from each magazine. Make pairs of cards from these by glueing them onto cardboard and covering them with clear contact paper. Then mix a bunch of these up, hold one up and ask, "Can you find one the *same* as this?" or "Look, I found a cat. Can you find a picture of a cat just like this?" Later the child will be able to play this independently.

You could also have children match pairs of identical small objects, fabric swatches, or paint samples.

Where to Find Pictures

Magazines, as mentioned, are the richest source. Old children's books that have been damaged can be recycled for toddler picture books. Favorite characters will be recognized in different positions, doing different things. Other sources: catalogues, sewing pattern books, photographs, junk mail.

Simple Picture Lotto

The only difference between a lotto game and matching cards is that lottos have several pictures on one larger board and individual pictures to match to the ones on the board. Make them the same way. Three or four pictures on the larger board will be enough for toddlers. You could take advantage of the game design and have a different "category" on each board. For instance, have 3 pictures of dogs on one, 3 cats on another, and 3 pictures of babies on a third board.

What Kind of Purchased Books Are Best for Toddlers and Twos?

We're talking about quite a wide range of language ability between the ages of 12 months and 3 years.

"Board books" rather than cloth books seem to be best for young toddlers. They can turn the pages more easily.

Picture books with one object or idea on a page are very good first books to start children naming objects. You should look for simplicity and clarity of illustrations and photographs, as well as their general attractiveness.

Children around 2 1/2 with slightly longer attention skills and expanding vocabulary like "busy" pictures with many different things on a page. It's fun to play the "Where is it?" game on page 80 with such books. There are several word books out like this that work well.

Finally, as children approach 3 they will be able to listen to very simple stories.

Young children seem to like animal characters. The people who write children's books are aware of this. Perhaps the child can identify with the animal stories easier than with people characters who are obviously not themselves. Young children are very ready to attribute human-like characteristics to things that are not human.

CHAPTER 8

How Things Work

Fitting Things Together

Toddlers like to put things inside of other things, match objects to holes, and make things stick. Commercial toys such as plastic blocks that fit together (make sure you get the kind that are too big for a child to choke on), nesting and stacking cups, and toys with small indentations in which to fit smaller items such as small wooden people appeal to toddlers for this reason. One fairly new such toy that has been greeted with much success with toddlers is "Wonder Blocks" by Mattel. They are easy for toddlers to handle, have rounded corners, and are made of a special kind of colorful plastic that is very appealing to the touch.

Puzzles

When children play with puzzles they develop an awareness of shapes and position, and the relationship of a single part to the whole picture. These are basic concepts for learning reading, writing and mathematics later. They are also developing coordination as they learn to fit a puzzle piece into its space.

As children approach two they will enjoy putting together simple wooden inlay puzzles. The simplest puzzles have one piece that fits into one hole, often with a knob to make pieces easier to pick up. Even such a simple puzzle can be surprisingly difficult for young toddlers because they must turn their wrist to make the puzzle piece fit. This is a new movement ability.

The next level of difficulty of puzzles is to have several pieces which each fit into their own individual hole on the same board. The child must then make a judgement about shapes and size to decide which piece to try in a given space.

More advanced puzzles have several pieces that fit into one larger space. To simplify such a puzzle you could glue several pieces in place with rubber cement. Later, as the child progresses, these pieces can be loosened to give the puzzle new challenge.

You can make simple puzzles for toddlers from heavy cardboard. Glue on a spool for a knob.

If you have access to a jigsaw it is simple to glue a picture to a small piece of wood and saw it into two or three pieces. Paint the picture with clear acrylic glaze for durability.

Shape Matching Game

Collect several small household objects such as jar lids, a coffee scoop, a comb, a plastic knife, and a canning ring. Trace around these objects on a piece of cardboard. Then let the child fit the objects into their space.

Spray Painted Shape Matching Game

Place a collection of small objects such as those described above on a piece of board or heavy cardboard. Then, simply spray paint over all of them. Spray paint dries very quickly. When it is dry, remove the objects and an unpainted silhouette will remain. The child then matches the object to the unpainted shape.

Nesting Toys

Here, our young scientists are discovering some basic principles of space and volume. They are learning that you can't fit something large into something smaller ... but how amazing, if you do it right you can fit all those smaller containers into one larger container! It's fun to watch the discovery. Give a child of about 1 year two plastic bowls of the same size and he will almost surely try to put one inside the other. His face shows excitement as he succeeds and does it again and again.

Bowls

The easiest type of nesting toy to give a young toddler is a set of bowls the same size. That way, success is much more likely.

Later the child will be eager to move on to nesting things of varied sizes. There are many things you could use. Large plastic food storage bowls that nest inside each other are ideal to start with because of their shape and size. Spray can tops, jar lids, margarine tubs and other household items also provide the toddler with a lot of variety to hold interest.

Cans

One of the most popular homemade toys for toddlers is a set of nesting cans made from increasing sizes of food cans. Make sure to file smooth any rough or sharp edges. Cover cans with contact paper to decorate them if you wish.

Canisters

An old set of kitchen canisters is a wonderful nesting toy for toddlers. Matching the lids to the correct canister is another challenge. They will also put small toys inside the canisters.

As children play with nesting toys they learn concepts of inside and outside, small, medium and large. Many nesting toys are also "stacking toys" giving them multiple uses and added interest.

Clothespins

A shoebox or can full of old-fashioned clothespins will occupy a toddler a long time. Show him how to make the clothespins straddle the edge of the box. Toddlers will also stick the clothespins together.

Spring-type clothespins are a more difficult challenge for older toddlers.

Stacking Things Up and Knocking Things Down

The stacking up is the challenging part and the knocking down is the fun part for toddlers. You can use anything safe such as sponges, wooden cubes or table blocks, cardboard blocks, cardboard boxes, milk cartons, spray can tops, corks, beanbags, or a combination of an odd assortment of these and other things.

There are fabric covered foam blocks in small and large sizes, and cardboard blocks on the market that are specially designed for toddlers. They are good because they are light and they are not likely to hurt the child if they fall down or are thrown.

Easy Milk Carton Blocks

Collect milk cartons of various sizes and wash them out thoroughly. Cut off the top point and fold down the top flaps to square off the box. Tape the edges. Cover the whole thing with pretty contact paper and the blocks will be surprisingly sturdy. In no time you will have a large collection of inexpensive and very satisfying blocks. Because they are so light, a toddler will not be hurt by a block that somehow becomes airborne.

Sturdier Milk Carton Blocks

Take two milk cartons of the same size, cut off the pointed ends, stuff one with newspaper and jam it inside of the other carton. Tape around the edge where they join with a strong tape.

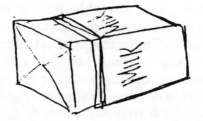

Grocery Bag Blocks

Let the toddler help you crumple newspaper to fill a paper grocery sack. When it is almost full, packed rather tightly, fold the top over to square off the end and tape it shut. Since these are big, and yet relatively light toddlers have fun lifting and stacking them. Because they are soft, nobody gets hurt when they topple down.

Sponges

It's fun to stack and knock down soft, dry sponges or chunks of foam rubber. The texture of sponges makes them slip less and toddlers experience more success stacking sponges than blocks at first. You might make a collection of 20 or 30 sponges in a box for toddlers to play with.

Playing with simple blocks and stacking toys gives children experience with some very basic problem solving and they learn simple lessons about balance.

Things That Spin

Kitchen Turntables

Your toddlers will have lots of fun with one of the plastic turntables designed for kitchen cabinets. The pure mechanics of making it spin around will grab their attention. Let them discover what happens if they put an object on the turntable and then spin it. You could tape a small toy to the edge and let the child give it a ride.

Cut out some magazine pictures and tape them to the turntable, and you have a word game. Cover these with clear contact paper if you want the pictures to stay around for a while. Let the child spin the turntable and then name the picture that stops in front of him.

Record Players

Toddlers enjoy a record player, not for the quality of the music it produces, although they no doubt like hearing the music, but mainly to watch the turntable go round and round. Do not invest in an expensive record player and records if you intend to allow the child to handle it. Several old records you scrounged at a garage sale or from friends and an inexpensive child's record player you picked up in the same way, or at a bargain store, will likely give your two year old much pleasure.

Record Player Art

Punch a hole in the middle of a paper plate and put it on the record player turntable. Give the child a felt tipped marking pen and show her how to move it back and forth on the paper plate as it revolves on the turntable. Pretty symmetrical patterns will result.

Spin Art

A commercial toy is available that spins a piece of paper around. Paint is put in the middle of the paper and the centrifugal force spreads it out in pleasing patterns. This is not really an art project for toddlers, because they don't really do anything in the process. They will, however, enjoy seeing the paper spin around and the colors spread out in pretty designs. You will have an opportunity to talk about colors.

Spinning Wheels

Although toddlers are too young to use a tricycle effectively, they greatly enjoy turning it upside down and spinning the wheels around. Add some pieces of paper to the wheels and a pretty visual pattern will emerge when the wheels spin around. They will also like spinning the wheels on their riding toys and scooters, toy cars, and trucks.

Spinning Top

One of the old-fashioned "pump" spinning tops is a good toy for toddlers, if you can find one. They will need help making it spin.

Turning Knobs and Screwing on Lids

Rotating their wrist is a new and difficult skill for toddlers. Some toys that are supposedly designed for toddlers, wind up music boxes in particular, are often too difficult for toddlers to wind themselves. What happens is the toddler follows the adult around, forever asking for the music box to be rewound. "Crank" type music box toys or Jack in the box type toys can also be difficult for toddlers to manipulate. There are some knobs, though, that toddlers are very successful at turning! One mother tells in dismay how her toddler son unscrewed all the knobs on the kitchen cabinets and drawers! Any toddler can turn the knob on the television, often to the consternation of the entire family, making it that much more fun.

Plastic Jar

Find a plastic jar with a lid small enough so that the toddler can get a grip on it easily. Put a few toys inside such as little wooden people or large plastic pop beads. See if the child can unscrew the lid and dump the toys out, replace the toys and screw the lid back on again. The mouth of the jar should be large enough so that the toddler can safely put his hand inside the jar without getting it stuck.

Knobs

Many "busy box" type toys for toddlers have simple knobs on them, usually connected with a sound that toddlers can manipulate.

Screw Top Board

Find 4 or 5 plastic bottles or jars with screw top lids of different sizes. Cut the bottles or jars off at the neck and nail them to a board. You may have to make cuts in the plastic in order for it to lie flat on the board. Children can practice screwing and unscrewing the tops, and they will have to match the correct size. For extra appeal, you might glue a texture inside that they can reach in with a finger and feel. You could spray paint the whole thing the same color to remove the color clue for matching.

This toy is too difficult for many toddlers but will attract interest from older two year olds.

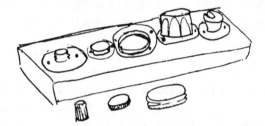

Peek-A-Boo

Young toddlers love activities that involve covering something up and uncovering it again or hiding something and quickly rediscovering it. Younger infants make the amazing discovery that something still exists even when they can no longer see it. Until about 6 months of age, if you hide an attractive toy under a blanket or behind a box, the infant will no longer look for it. "Out of sight, out of mind." But after that, the child will push the box aside or pull the blanket to retrieve the toy, indicating that there was still a mental image of the toy when it was out of sight. Toddlers still love to "test" this. A spontaneous game of peek-a-boo will often turn a cranky and fussing toddler into a giggling child.

Classical Peek-A-Boo

Put your hands in front of your face. Open them out like the doors on a cuckoo clock and say, "peek-a-boo" and close them

again. Do this repeatedly and you will get the smiles and attention of young toddlers. Best of all, you can probably get the toddler
to do it too. "Now you do it."

A thin scarf held in front of the child's face and quickly pulled
away will be a favorite. Toddlers have often been seen to do this
with clothing, their coats, security blankets, and bedding. Many
toddlers do not like clothing that must be pulled over their
heads—even undershirts. Saying "peek-a-boo" when the head
pops out may diffuse the anger.

Popping up and down from behind a chair or shelf is also fun.
Children quickly learn to do this themselves. This may be one of
the first forms of social interactions between children of the same
age. Puppets, teddy bears and dolls are, of course, also very good
at playing peek-a-boo.

Pop Up Stick Puppet

Poke a hole in the bottom of a paper or plastic cup. Fit a
plastic drinking straw or wooden dowel through the hole. Attach
a small toy or a face on a small ball to the end of the dowel so that
it can pop in and out of the cup when you move the dowel. There
are many ways you could elaborate this simple puppet.

Glove Pop Up Puppet

You need an old glove (inexpensive garden gloves work well), a dowel about 2 feet long, and fabric to form a tube around the dowel for the puppet's body. Use a small styrofoam or other ball for the head and yarn, felt and other scraps for features and hair. Sew the bottom of the fabric tube to the top of the second and third fingers of the glove, as illustrated. Push the dowel through the tube and attach the head on the end. Make the puppet pop up and down by pushing the dowel up and down. In addition to playing peek-a-boo, this puppet could talk to children, tickle their chin, etc.

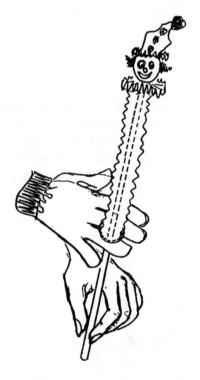

Mirror with a Curtain

Rig up a curtain over a mirror. (It's always good to have a low mirror where toddlers can see themselves.) The child will enjoy pulling the curtain aside and saying "Peek-a-boo" to his own image.

Doll Blankets

One of the things toddlers most often do with dolls, given the opportunity, is to cover and uncover the doll with a small blanket. This is a form of a peek-a-boo game for toddlers.

Books

When you think about it, turning the pages of books is a form of a peek-a-boo activity. Watch a toddler with a book for a few minutes — it's the "mechanics" of the book that first intrigue the child. Turn the page — the picture goes away — then turn it back and it appears again! (This "reversibility learning" is one step toward the development of logical reasoning much later in life.) You will notice that toddlers often turn the same pages back and forth, back and forth. This is one reason it makes sense to have books around that toddlers are allowed to handle themselves.

Suitcases

A small suitcase or briefcase is an ideal thing to put with other dramatic play materials for toddlers. They will love packing and unpacking it and lugging it around. Part of the appeal of playing with a suitcase is to discover that the things inside are still there when the suitcase is opened up again. They will also be fascinated with the latches.

Peek-A-Boo Books

These are the books that have little doors to open on the pages to reveal something underneath. You could also make books like these from cloth or cardboard. Toddlers love these kinds of books, but they should probably be used exclusively on an adult's lap because toddlers also tend to tear the flaps off. Other books have little pockets in them to put things in. There are elaborate "pop-out" books where 3 dimensional things appear when pages are opened.

Peek-A-Boo Guessing Book

Use a small spiral notebook for this. You can get index cards that are spiral bound that are especially good for this. Glue a full page picture of a familiar object or scene to every other page, starting with the second page. Cover all the pages on both sides with clear contact paper. Cut the pages with no pictures on them into several horizontal strips, going from the edge of the page over to the spiral binding.

When you look at this book with the child, turn one strip at a time, gradually revealing more and more of the picture underneath. Let the child guess what the picture is.

Peek-A-Boo Puzzles

These are wooden inlay puzzles with individual pieces with knobs on them to make them easier for small hands to remove. Under each puzzle piece is another picture. This adds motivation and appeal to the puzzle. A child is usually approaching two before she can work such a puzzle without help. These puzzles usually cost about $10.

The Old Shell Game

Take three containers — cans or stocking eggs halves would work nicely — and put a small toy under one. Move them slowly to change their positions while the child watches. Can he pick the one that has the toy under it?

Bury Things in the Sand Box

Sit down next to the toddler in the sandbox and show him how to dig a small hole, put a small object in it and cover it up with sand again. Then ask, "Where's the *car*?" When the child removes the sand to uncover the object express delight: "There's the car!"

Unwrapping Things

Taking the paper off presents, opening boxes, finding "surprises" in shopping bags, even peeling oranges, eggs or bananas have an element of "peek-a-boo".

Latch and Lock Board

These can be purchased from school supply catalogues or toy stores. They are a very popular toy because toddlers love to manipulate small things with their fingers. They also enjoy the hinge effect of the little doors. If you add little pictures or a mirror behind the doors you will add the peek-a-boo appeal. Note: Sometimes such lock and latch boards are not well made and fall apart, leaving small sharp nails to hurt toddlers. Keep them in good repair, or, better yet, make your own.

A Simple Door Board

Two large pieces of posterboard, some glue and some magazine pictures are all you need for this. Cut a number of little doors in one piece of posterboard. Place this over the second piece of posterboard and trace around the holes where the doors are. Remove the top board and glue magazine pictures in the spaces traced from the door holes. Then glue the top piece of posterboard with the doors onto the bottom piece. Children will love to open the little doors to see what's underneath. You could attach a little loop of yarn to make the door easier to open.

Advent Calendars

These are traditional calendars used to count down the days before Christmas, made much like the door board described above. You could actually make one of these to anticipate any coming event such as a birthday, a trip to the zoo or when daddy comes home from a business trip. There is a numbered door for each waiting day. The child opens one door each day. There is a topic related picture under each door. In addition to the fun of revealing pictures under the doors, it may begin to give the child a feeling for the passage of time and what a day and a week is ... although full understanding of time will not come for several years. Older children will get practice using numbers in the correct sequence.

Match Boxes

Small match boxes with the little "drawers" that slide out fascinate toddlers both because of mechanics and because of what's inside of them. Remove the matches. One teacher I knew glued different textures of materials inside the drawers: cotton, sandpaper, chamois, sponge, etc. You could also glue attractive pictures into the match box drawers. Reinforcing the outside of the match box with pretty contact paper will also increase its durability. It's fun because the toddler can make the thing inside appear and disappear by pushing the drawer in and out.

Toddler Hide and Seek

This is a thrilling game greatly enjoyed by toddlers. When children aren't looking, simply hide yourself and call out, "I'm hiding . . . come and find me!" Leave part of you sticking out and visible. Children will learn to follow the direction of your voice. Do they associate one visible shoulder and arm with the whole body attached to it? What a thrill when they find you . . . a good excuse for a hug! Eventually you can invite a child to hide herself. Does she know what it means? Sometimes the child will think she is hiding but is almost completely visible to other children. To hide successfully a child must develop a sense of the space of her own body and must also start to think about how something would look from someone else's point of view . . . very difficult for toddlers. An adult will probably have to help the toddler hide.

Who's Under the Sheet?

Have children close their eyes or turn their backs and cover up one child with a small sheet or blanket. Then let the others feel the sheet and try to guess who is under it. You can give clues by exposing a shoe, part of the hair, etc. This game is more difficult than it may seem. Children have to maintain a mental image of the other child. It works only when all the children know each other well, and when children are at least 2½. Even if it's not totally successful, it's still fun being under the sheet and being the center of attention!

Hide a Toy

When children come in from outside, or wake up from naps (or anytime) you might say, "I have hidden Teddy Bear. Can you find him?" Leave part visible. They have to remember what the toy looks like and must use a certain amount of reasoning in the process.

Poking Things and Fingers Through Holes

Show any toddler a surface with holes in it and she will immediately stick a finger in the hole! My guess is that it has something to do with "object permanence" — learning that something continues to exist even if one can't see it. Probably there's also some fascination with their developing eye-hand coordination — that they can make something go exactly where they want it to go, and fitting things together. "What will my finger fit into?" This compulsion is what makes electrical outlets so dangerous in a toddler environment. Make sure you put safety caps on all of your outlets.

There are many good commercial toys that allow toddlers to practice this compulsion. School supply companies (see appendix) carry large rubber pegboards with either 25 or 100 holes in them. "Easy-Grip Pegs" are 2½" colorful, knoblike plastic pegs that fit into these holes. This toy gets good concentration from toddlers as they get practice in eye-hand coordination. There are also other toys that involve putting wooden cylinders into holes. Shape sorting boxes are also good for this purpose. The popular Snap-Lock beads by Fischer Price involve sticking something in a hole. Toddlers also like to put their fingers into these holes.

With toys that have pieces, make sure the pieces are not small enough for toddlers to choke on or shove into their ears or nostrils (the ever-present, most convenient holes!) For this reason, many fine toys for preschoolers such as small wooden pegs, small beads, small fit together toys, etc. are not appropriate for toddlers.

Shape Sorting Boxes

These are very popular commercial toys marketed to parents of toddlers. They are often a bit hard for toddlers. Make an easier

version yourself by cutting a round hole in a plastic coffee can lid or a shoebox lid. Save the caps from plastic milk jugs and let the child drop them through the hole. Children will also like stuffing larger pieces of foam rubber through the hole.

Plunker

Cut an X in the plastic lid of a coffee can or margarine tub. Let the child push wooden beads (or milk jug lids or some other such thing) through the X. They will love the plunking noise it makes. You could make a color sorter by spray painting several coffee cans different colors or covering them with colored contact paper. Then tell the child to put wooden beads the *same* color as this in this can. They may not get the idea because "color" is an abstract concept — so don't get frustrated. Your pet puppet could help.

Slot Boxes for Clean Up

Use a "boutique" type tissue box for crayon storage. Toddlers love to drop the crayons through the slot to put them away and reach in to get another.

You could use the cardboard grocery cartons that already have a slot in the lid, or cut a hole or slot in the top of a box. Have children stick pieces of table toys through the slot. Provide a different box for each toy.

Plastic Bottle Plunker

Cut a door at the base of a bleach bottle or other large plastic bottle. Let the child stick things through the mouth of the bottle and take them out of the door at the bottom.

Bleach Bottle Sorter

Cut 3 X's or holes in the side of a plastic bleach bottle and surround these with 3 different colors. (Permanent ink felt markers work.) Have children stick various colored objects through the matching hole. Large, "Easy-Grip" pegs, teddy bear counters, milk jug tops, poker chips, plastic clothespins and large wooden beads are possibilities. Have a "back door' cut to remove the objects.

Holey Book

Make a homemade book from cloth or heavy cardboard with holes in the pictures for children to stick their fingers through from behind. Ideas: an apple with a worm hole; a ballerina with 2 holes for legs; a little girl with holes for pigtails; a doggie with 4 holes for legs; an elephant with a hole for a trunk.

Stringing Beads

The appeal of stringing beads to toddlers is actually that of poking something through a hole.

The traditional beads and laces you can buy are often too difficult for two year olds because the laces are soft and floppy. They are challenging for 3½ year olds. Large, brightly colored wooden beads are a good size for twos to handle. Use thin plastic tubing (like aquarium tubing) instead of the laces that come with the beads, and two year olds will find more success.

Empty thread spools are good for stringing too.

Later, children will enjoy stringing O-shaped cereal onto shoelaces.

Stacking Rings

This is another popular commercial toy for toddlers. Toddlers usually pay little attention to the relative size of the rings, nor

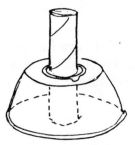

will they always put them on in order. The appeal is putting the stick through the hole in the ring. Here are some homemade variations:

Large wooden curtain rings can be placed over a stick.

Rubber canning rings can be fit over a can or cardboard cylinder attached to a base, such as an inverted margarine tub.

Feed the Wastebasket

Get one of those large waste containers with a cover and flap door. Make a face around it so the door is the mouth. Children will love to feed it napkins after snack time and lunch time.

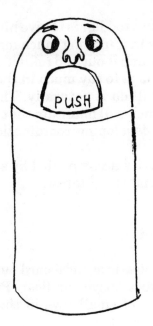

Bracelets

Colored plastic bracelets are fun to have for toddlers. They love putting their hand through them and walking around the room with their arms extended.

6 Packs

Toddlers like to put small toys in cardboard 6-pack containers and carry them around.

Liquor Boxes

Get the kind of box from a liquor store that has individual compartments for the bottles. Collect some paper towel tubes, or empty plastic bottles. Let the child put the tubes or bottles into the compartments.

Emptying and Filling

One way to occupy a toddler is to give him a container of some sort with some objects in it (doesn't much matter what, as long as it's safe) and let him dump it out and refill it again and again. You probably won't even have to say much in the way of an introduction ... the toddler will do it naturally. There are many variations to this theme which will maintain the child's interest. In the process, the child is developing coordination of hand and arm muscles.

The magic of gravity accompanied by satisfying "cause and effect" noises compound the interest.

Fill and Spill Bucket

Suspend a small plastic or cardboard bucket from the ceiling so it hangs about a foot above the floor. Put a plastic dishpan under it. Put a bunch of small toys in the dishpan. Show the

toddler how to put the toys from the dishpan into the bucket, and then dump them back into the dishpan. Toddlers like to do this over and over again.

Toy Transfer Game

Put two dishpans on opposite sides of the room. Fill one with small toys. Provide a container with a handle that is fun to carry such as a colorful Easter basket. Show the child how to load the toys into the Easter basket, carry them across the room and dump them into the empty dishpan. Then, of course, the child can transfer the toys back to the first dishpan in the same way. As the child enjoys this activity over and over, you can talk about concepts of "empty" and "full".

Margarine Tubs with Toys Inside

Although it may be difficult at first, toddlers like to peel the plastic lids off margarine tubs. If there are small toys inside such as large wooden beads, or little wooden people, there will be even more incentive.

Chain and Bottle

Get a short length of chain with smallish links. First give it to the child to put in a margarine tub. Later, see if the child can put it into a plastic bottle with a small mouth. This is more complex than it may seem. Don't show the child how to do it. Let her figure it out herself. Does she feed it in one link at a time? Does she give up? Does she figure out how to dangle it over the bottle and drop it in all at once?

Large Wooden Beads or Wooden People and an Ice Cube Tray or Egg Carton

The child will enjoy putting one thing in each space. Being able to close the lid on the egg carton adds another dimension. You could tie a piece of yarn to one end and make it into a pull toy. Tie *several* together and make a train!

Pour a Bead

Give a child two containers such as plastic glasses and one large wooden bead. Let the child "pour" the bead from one glass to the other.

Sand and Water Play

Filling and pouring are, of course, major concentrations in sand and water play. Just concentrate on giving the toddler a wide variety of containers to use. Spray can tops give you much variety in size and color and are fun to use.

Puppet Game with a Box of Junk

Since a toddler will do almost anything for a puppet, you can use your puppet to help the child empty or fill a container and talk about what is happening. The puppet may ask the child to find some specific things in the room to put in the container. This is a very effective tool to use if you want the toddler's help in cleaning up.

Travel Kit Toys

Soap Box Cards

Find a plastic soap box such as those used in travel cases. Put a deck of playing cards inside. When the cards are dumped it is quite a challenge to get them all back in because they have to be turned in the right direction. The lid must also be positioned correctly to fit back on.

Toothbrush Holder and Popsicle Sticks

Put several popsicle sticks (or craft sticks, as they are sometimes called) in a plastic toothbrush holder. It is a different kind of challenge getting the end of the stick into the narrow opening at the end of the long plastic box.

Small Flat Travel Jars

These can be filled with cotton balls for the toddler to put in and out.

Zipper Case

The zippered travel case is itself a valuable container for the above treasures, and the child will like to zip and unzip it.

CHAPTER 9

Different Ways
of Moving

Climbing

Toddlers are compulsive climbers. They will scale anything available including bookshelves, chairs and tables. For the safety of life and limb as well as the preservation of furniture, it is highly desirable to provide children with something legitimate to climb.

This is one instance where the purchase of one of the many available manufactured climbing apparatuses is advisable because of the durable and safe construction offered by manufacturers.

Rocking Boat

The popular "rocking boat" that turns over into a set of stairs is a good piece, and it has the advantage of multiple uses. It is safely built to be stable and when used as a rocking boat it will not tip over. Children often will sing "Row, row, row your boat" (or a version thereof) if the teacher has sung this as they rock. If the adult talks about what the child is doing as he goes up and down the steps "Johnny is stepping up ... now he is stepping down ..." the child gains vocabulary advances as well as physical skill. Be careful that fingers don't get pinched.

Toddler Slide

This is the little platform with two steps leading up to it and a small slide going down the other side. The child gets practice climbing stairs as well as the fun of sliding down the short slide. The space under the slide seems to be most popular of all. Children crawl through the circle and enjoy huddling in the enclosed space under the platform. This costs about $80.

Nautilus

This molded plastic piece also provides opportunities for climbing, sliding and crawling into an enclosed space. It has the advantages of great stability, no moveable parts, no sharp edges, and virtual indestructibility. It is made by Learning Products, Inc. costs about $120 and is available from most toy suppliers (see appendix).

Jungle Gyms

There are numerous "transitional" climbing structures that are appropriate for older preschoolers but only safe for toddlers if an adult is close at hand. They do provide great challenge and pleasure for toddlers. Some climbers fold flat fairly easily, allowing teachers to put them away, setting them up only when close supervision is possible. Put any climber over a soft surface.

If a child becomes "stuck" or afraid to climb down, resist the temptation to simply "rescue" him and lift him off. Instead, try to show the child how to do it himself. You can put your hand on his hand or foot and guide it to a lower rung — step by step. "Oh — I see you are stuck, Nicole. Here. Put this foot down here. That's right! Now put this hand over here. This hand here now. Can you get down the rest of the way now? Good! You did it yourself." Instead of being a temporary solution you are thus helping the child develop skills and confidence. This approach is much more helpful to the child in the long run.

Stairs

Young toddlers especially, or infants just learning to walk are fascinated by stairs. It's important that you keep a gate across stairs to prevent falls. When you can, spend some time with a toddler on some stairs. Let the child enjoy the challenge of going up step after step with you right behind for safety. It is much harder for a toddler to go down stairs than to climb up. Show him how to crawl down backwards on his tummy. This is one thing a child can be taught to do, often earlier than he would have discovered it on his own and this skill may prevent some nasty falls.

A toddler will gradually learn to go up and down stairs in an upright posture, one step at a time. Children don't usually alternate feet going up and down stairs until well after their third birthday.

Crawling and Hiding in Small Places

Why do toddlers like to be in and under things so much? Is it the comfortable memory of the prenatal period? We will never know! Undoubtedly as a child fits himself into a small space he is developing a sense of his own body and how much space he takes up. The concepts of in, out, under, through, behind . . . are slowly being absorbed as adults talk, and the child is getting needed exercise.

Tunnels

Purchased fabric tunnels are very popular in toddler programs. Playground tunnels are often made of large concrete pipe, metal barrels, several tires stood up on end and bolted together side by side, or square wooden tunnels, carpeted with indoor/outdoor carpeting. You can make a tunnel by removing the ends from cardboard grocery boxes and taping or lacing a number of boxes together end to end. It won't last forever, but it's free and should provide you with several days of fun.

Patchwork Playhouse

A teacher I knew a long time ago made this type of playhouse for her toddler room and it survived for at least the two years I was in and out of her classroom. Starting with a large carton a washing machine came in, she cut a door that would open and close and a window and left the flaps on for shutters. Then she glued upholstery samples all over the outside and painted over it with an acrylic polymer glaze (which is partly what made the playhouse so sturdy.) Carpet samples went on the floor inside. This playhouse was always occupied by several toddlers at once.

Boxes

Collect a bunch of cardboard grocery cartons. Simply put them in the room with toddlers and watch the fun.

Toddlers also enjoy sitting in plastic dish tubs, galvanized wash tubs, an empty shelf unit you have laid on its side, — any large container. In fact, not having an accurate sense of the size of their body, they will also try to get into sand pails, mixing bowls, and other containers which are far too small for them.

A Counter Cave

One teacher removed two cabinet doors under a counter. She removed the shelves and placed a small foam mattress and some pillows inside. Children enjoy crawling into this cozy spot.

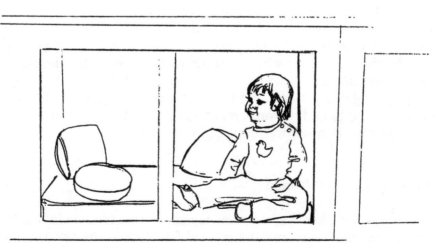

Table Skirts

Another teacher sewed fabric skirts to fit around low tables (not unlike the cardtable cover "playhouses" you can buy). This gives children several hide-away spots in her room.

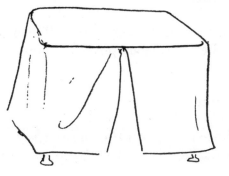

Obstacle Course

Make an obstacle course in your room by making a line of masking tape or yarn to follow over chairs, under tables, around and behind shelves, pillows, etc. Demonstrate what to do and have children follow you. This is great to do on a bad weather day when you can't go outside and want to provide some exercise and diversity.

Running and Falling

Slap-stick humor has obvious appeal to toddlers, and running and purposely falling down seems to be a popular way toddlers get other children to laugh.

Ring Around the Rosie

The obvious appeal of this song is falling down. It does not necessarily have to be a "rosie" that you ring around. You can ring around the pumpkin, a Christmas tree, a valentine, an Easter bunny, etc. No matter, toddlers will always enjoy the game.

Record Player Cue

Dance while the music plays, fall down when it stops.

Pile Up on Teacher

Nothing is more fun than crawling all over a favorite adult who is lying on the floor. Good physical contact.

Follow the Leader

Children like to incorporate falling and getting up into follow the leader games.

The Chase Game

Much to a hurried parent's frustration, toddlers love to chase and be chased. If you make a legitimate game out of it perhaps you can say later when running away is not appropriate, "We're not playing chase now." To play, say "You chase me — I'm running away from you. Oh, no! You caught me! Now I'll chase you!"

Diving into a Pile of Pillows

This game will require no instruction. Just provide a corner full of pillows and it will happen spontaneously.

Going Around Something

Toddlers like to walk, run, jump, *around* a large object like a tree, a bush, a table, a chair, or another child. I've often seen toddlers do this spontaneously. One child will move a chair to a central spot and simply start walking around it. Often she is joined by one or two other children. Perhaps having a focal point object in the middle makes it easier to circle around and get back to where you started from. Perhaps it starts with children wanting to see what something looks like from the other side. Usually all you have to do is put on a record (even that is not really necessary) and say, "Let's walk around the table," and around they'll go. In the process they are learning what "around" means as well as seeing their environment from different perspectives.

Throwing

Toddlers love to throw things. It's probably a fascination with the cause and effect phenomenon — pure physics. "I make my arm do this, release at the proper moment, and the thing goes flying through the air. Wonderful!"

Stuff to Throw Box

The obvious thing is to have objects available that are okay to throw so you can redirect when children throw inappropriate things. Possibilities: bean bags (keep in good repair), yarn balls, soft sponges (watch for eating), soft "clutch balls", crocheted toys, nerf balls, stuffed animals, fabric covered foam blocks, small brown bags stuffed with wadded up newspaper, taped shut.

Targets

You might block off a corner of the room and challenge children to throw the things you give them into that corner. A laundry basket or a large cardboard box make good targets too.

Pushing Things

Very often the most popular purchased toy in the room is the little shopping cart bought at a variety store. (They do seem fairly durable.) Toddlers push them around endlessly, and they enjoy filling and emptying the basket too. One often sees toddlers pushing their own strollers in shopping malls. POWER!

Train

Have children push a bunch of chairs together to make a train or bus. This activity is a sure hit.

Push a Friend on a Riding Toy

Toddlers like to give their friends a ride by pushing a riding toy. It's as much fun as being the rider. A good way to learn about taking turns.

Pushing Boxes

If you provide empty grocery boxes, toddlers often choose to push them around the room. They could give a doll a ride.

Toy Vehicles

Toy cars and trucks get much attention from toddlers. It's best to get durable toy vehicles because toddlers will try to sit on or in them, even if they are way too big. Make sure wheels are securely attached.

Trains are especially interesting to toddlers.

I've noticed that children especially enjoy pushing toy vehicles along a ledge in a room such as a radiator or a shelf.

Push Toys

Commercially available push toys on the end of a stick remain popular with toddlers. These toys usually include a sound consequence which give children the added pleasure of a "cause and effect" response. Much of the appeal is also in imitating adults pushing a vacuum cleaner or mop.

Roll a Ball Back and Forth

With either two of you or a small group of children teach them to *push* the ball to make it roll. See if they can eventually gain control over the direction and roll it to a specific person or place.

Drawers

Opening and closing drawers fascinate children for this reason. It's nice to have one drawer set aside that is allowable for children to open and close.

Sliding and Rolling

A short slide is very exciting to toddlers. Children will seem to do a survey on how many ways one can go down a slide. Physics, gravity, and body awareness are experienced.

At Pacific Oaks College's Toddler Yard in Pasadena, they have used a sheet of formica 4' wide for the surface of the slide. If children should flop over there is less danger, and the surface does not get intolerably hot in the warm weather of Southern California.

Rolling Things Down a Slide

You can put a box at the bottom of a slide and let children roll things down the slide and into the box. Toddlers like to watch toys go down a slide.

Rolling

It's hard for toddlers to lie on their side and roll over and over. Lateral torso muscles get new practice. Rolling down a grassy hill at the park is wonderful fun. But it's fun just rolling on the floor too.

Rolling cans and cylinders is fun.

Wagon

A small wagon is a good toy for twos. They push it, pull it, load and unload it and give toys and each other rides in it.

Different Ways of Moving

Walk the Plank

Find a board about 8 to 12 inches wide and about 4 feet long. Place it flat on the floor. Challenge the child to walk all the way across it without stepping off. Try other ways of moving along the plank. Crawling should be easy. Older two year olds may be able to tip-toe across, step sideways, or even walk backwards.

To add challenge to the activity raise the plank a few inches by putting a sturdy block or brick under each end. Kneel nearby to steady the child if necessary.

Children are gaining skill in balance and general coordination.

Follow the Leader Moves

Using the "follow the leader" technique, model for the child or children different ways to move. They will imitate you. Try: crawling, jumping, rolling, walking, walking on tip toe, sliding sideways, dancing, waving your arms. You can add music. The beauty of this activity is it is immediately available, and children will always join you. It's irresistible. *Creative Movement for the Developing Child* (see appendix) is a small book that describes many movement activities good for children over 2 1/2, often combining poetry and imitating animals.

Jumping

Once toddlers master standing and walking it seems that their next logical goal is to learn how to fly! Anyway, they sure jump a lot. In an attempt to jump, they don't always get completely off the ground, but they try. Here are some simple and fun jumping activities.

Jingle Bell Anklets

Sew some jingle bells onto elastic that will fit a child's ankles comfortably. They love to jump up and down to music on the record player and make the jingle bells ring.

Hold Hands and Jump

Simple as it seems, this activity is a real winner! Just hold hands with a child and jump up and down—with or without music. You could chant, "Jump, jump, jump ..." You could do this with several children at once in a circle.

Greeting Song

Have children sit in a circle (or a reasonable facsimile thereof). One child at a time jumps up and down in the middle of the circle as the others sing and clap:

"*Jenny's* here today,
Jenny's here today,
We all clap together 'cause,
Jenny's here today."

Substitute each child's name, and sing to the tune of "Farmer in the Dell."

Jump Off a Low Platform

Have you noticed how toddlers like to jump off the bottom step of the stairs, or from railroad ties on the playground? You could build a small wooden platform about six inches high for inside. Carpet it perhaps. They'll use it a lot!

Folk Songs

Traditional songs — like "Jim Along Josie" and "Clap, Clap, Clap Your Hands" and undoubtedly many others involve jumping movements — or make up your own jumping songs. *American Folk Songs for Children* (see appendix) has many good activity songs.

Mattress

Place an old mattress on the floor covered with a sheet and allow children to jump up and down on it. Great fun!

Inner Tube

If you can find a large truck inner tube children, several at a time, will have fun straddling it and bouncing up and down.

Knee Bounce

Don't forget the simple pleasure of bouncing a child on your knee. Toddlers still love this! Combine it with simple "bouncing rhymes". Rhythm, balance and good physical contact with an adult are the benefits. In case you have forgotten the rhymes from your childhood, here are a couple. (Of course, you could really use any lively rhyme, or make up your own.)

To market, to market to buy a fat pig
Home again, home again, jiggety-jig.
To market, to market to buy a fat hog
Home again, home again jiggety jog.

Ride a cock horse
To Banbury Cross,
To see a fine lady
Upon a white horse.
With rings on her fingers
And bells on her toes,
She shall have music
Wherever she goes.

(From the Puffin Book of Nursery Rhymes.)

Dancing

Put some music on and it's hard to *keep* toddlers from dancing! If you dance too and move in different ways your toddlers will dance even more. In the process they practice balance, coordination, and rhythm and experience the pure pleasure of moving to music.

"The Toddler Stomp"

The typical toddler "dance" is to rock side to side in a wide stance.

Children often start doing this spontaneously when they hear some lively music. They also enjoy doing the "toddler stomp" holding hands with a partner. Good social interaction.

Hip Dancing

What toddlers love most of all is for an adult to pick them up, sit them on their hip and dance to music.

Swinging

Toddlers love to swing and they are learning more physics as they do so. Centrifugal force and gravity are felt with their whole body. Swings with soft "sling" seats and horizontal tire swings are safest for toddlers.

Swings need close adult supervision. Toddlers have absolutely no sense of the amount of space swings require and will walk right in front of them. It is a good idea to hang swings up over the top bar of the swing when they cannot be closely supervised.

One favorite activity is to swing back and forth, tummy down.

Pendulums

Toddlers also enjoy playing with simple pendulums. Tie a bean bag to a short string and let the child dangle it back and forth. Keep an eye on this so the string doesn't accidentally get around the child's neck. Put it away when you're not supervising.

Riding Toys

Although tricycles are too advanced for many toddlers, they greatly enjoy wheeled riding toys, propelling them with their feet on the ground. These toys work well indoors and outdoors. When children ride these little scooters and cars and trucks they are involved in valuable dramatic play while developing the coordination to later succeed with the pedals of a tricycle.

Some teachers have devised high peg board hangers so they can put riding toys up when the room cannot tolerate heavy vehicular traffic.

You might try marking off a "road" on the floor, to cut down on reckless driving. This also provides the added challenge of steering the toy to stay within certain boundaries.

Learning Products, Inc. makes a variety of very durable and attractive molded plastic riding toys ranging in price from $30 to $40. Wooden riding toys are available from toy suppliers at comparable costs. (See appendix.)

Stick Horses

Toddlers have a good time cavorting around the yard on stick horses and you can make lovely ones from stuffed socks, or even stuffed paper bags attached to thick dowels or cut up broom handles, available from a hardware store. Because toddlers also enjoy swinging these horses around like bats or doing harm to their fellow man by poking, you may have to bring these horses out only when you can ride with them and then herd them back into the corral.

CHAPTER 10

Teaching Strategies to Help with Special Problems of Toddlers in Groups

This chapter addresses primarily people who are involved in supervising groups of toddlers. Parents will find relevance, however, when neighborhood children or relatives visit, or whenever there is more than one preschool child in the room, even siblings.

I am listing problems I most commonly hear voiced by teachers. The solutions also come from toddler teachers.

Toddlers Vacillate Between Clinging and Wanting Independence

"I wanna do it *myself!*" Not surprising that this is often one of the first full sentences uttered by young children! At this exciting age when they are suddenly mobile and have the growing skill of language they are discovering their power as independent human beings. Naturally, they have to test their power, often leading to insurrections and "civil disobedience." What sometimes confuses people is that it is often only minutes later that this same independent, venturesome child is back crawling on your lap, clinging to your leg, or asking for help in something she can do herself.

Toddlers need to keep checking the security of their base before they venture out. The secure base is the parent or other caring adult with whom the child has a trusting relationship.

In all of these discussions on activities and learning let me not neglect to mention the importance of cuddling, rocking, stroking and hugging toddlers.

Children at home often have more opportunities to act independently than children in group care. There are many ways we can offer toddlers the choice of more power and independence in their environment. Naturally, there are many times when a young child must do what the adult wishes whether he wants to or not — like putting on boots in wet weather or putting away toys at a certain time, for that matter. I am not in any way advocating a completely permissive atmosphere in which children can do whatever they want all day. We all know what that would look like. But it might be good to consider how we can design the program to allow toddlers as many legitimate choices and opportunities to affect their environment as possible.

What *can* toddlers do for themselves and what real decisions can you engineer for them? Here are some starting ideas for you:

1. When a child produces a work of art let the child decide where to hang it. Simply put a piece of tape on it and let the child put it up. (You can take it down to send home after a day or two.)
2. Instead of sitting everyone down at the table for an art project at the same time, simply announce, "I've got some paint and sponges and paper over at the table for anyone who wants to paint. Susie will be over there to help you if you decide to do that. It'll be there all morning." As the morning progresses Susie can invite individuals to paint when space becomes available and children should be allowed to decline.
3. "Would you like orange slices or apple slices for snack? or both?" (Hint: usually, when you offer toddlers a choice, they will choose the last thing you mentioned.)
4. With self-help routines, children can learn to wash their own hands, take off and put on their own socks and shoes, take care of most of their own toilet routines, get a drink, hang up their coat, wash their face, etc. Encourage parents to dress their children in clothing that is easy for children to put on and off themselves.

5. Children enjoy helping with basic routines. Setting the table, handing out napkins, clearing dishes, setting out mats at naptime, putting away toys, turning off lights, handing out paper and art supplies, washing brushes, etc., are all things children can help with. Sure, it takes a little longer. Justify the time by considering this part of your basic curriculum.

6. Ask children's advice and opinions when you're prepared to go with their choices. "Do you think we ought to go outside now or shall we wait till after snack?" "Which record shall I put on for naptime?" "Shall we put out the clay or the playdough on that table?" "Do you feel like playing with water today?" "Shall we have snack outside or inside today?" "Do you want yellow or blue?"

7. Allow things to happen. Notice children's spontaneous play activities and expand on them. When you hear some spontaneous singing, join in. Repeat children's nonsense syllable chants. When someone starts dancing to music get others to do it too.

8. Allow children not to participate—don't feel they have to function as a group all the time. Work it out with other staff, who will supervise a special project and who will keep an eye on the rest of the group. Then just plunk yourself down and start doing something, like finding pictures in a magazine, rolling a ball or reading a story. The ones who are interested and developmentally ready for the activity will gravitate over to you sooner or later.

Again, please forgive if this sounds "laissez-faire". Certainly there are times when you will need to expedite. Just get in the habit of asking yourself, "Is it important that children do it my way right now, or can I allow them the choice?" Common sense will lead you to the right balance.

Toddlers Won't Share and They Fight Over Toys

"Mine!" The cry of toddlerhood! Sharing is hardly even an "emerging skill" for toddlers. The territorial imperative is often what leads to outbreaks of violence. We've all seen toddlers who rigorously defend every toy at home, howling in protest if another child touches one. And we've all seen toddlers who insist on grabbing another child's toy even though there's a whole room full of perfectly good toys no one is using. There is a long road in front of you. It takes a long time and many gently guided experiences to learn to share. Very gradually it will sink in.

Paul and the Ball

Here is a true scenario very typical of toddlers:

Paul is a new child in the Toddler House. It's his third day there and he's doing okay, although not talking much. He spots a ball on a shelf in the bathroom, points to it and shouts, "Ball!" The teacher takes it down and puts it in the room for the children to play with. Another older, larger child immediately grabs the ball, runs to the rocking boat, puts it in and sits on it, making sure Paul cannot touch it. (Pecking order being established.) The teacher suggests the children sit in a circle with her and have fun rolling the ball to each other. The enticement of the teacher as a play-mate gets cooperation. About 6 children choose to join her, including the ball possessor. She holds out her hands and says, "Roll me the ball!" Paul's face shows great anticipation. The ball is rolled back and forth between children. The second time the teacher gets the ball she rolls it to Paul. He grabs it eagerly and holds it. Everyone looks at him. The teacher holds her hands out. "Roll me the ball, Paul!" No response. The other children hold their hands out. "Ball!" Paul hangs on. "We'll roll it right back to you!" He *cannot* let go of the ball. Clearly, this is an issue of trust. The teacher decides not to take the ball away from him. "It looks like Paul needs to hold that ball now. Let's toss this foam block to each other instead." That sounds good to the other kids and they throw the soft block back and forth, grabbing it if it lands near them. After a few minutes, lo and behold, Paul rolls the ball to the teacher! She rolls the ball back to him immediately, and claps when he gets it, holds her hands out expectantly and he rolls it back. She sends it right back to him and claps. He rolls it back. She then rolls it to someone else, and the game continues a few minutes more with everyone clapping when someone caught the ball. Paul had to give up the ball on his own terms. Slowly the foundations of trust were being developed.

The same morning another child, Maria, comes in clutching

a small box of raisins. This happens every morning. She is a shy child and her mother feels the raisins will help give her social entree. Maria magnanimously hands out one or two raisins to children who cluster around her. Everyone smiles. A little while later she stumbles and drops the raisins which spill out of the box. All activity in the room stops and heads turn toward her. She screams and desperately tries to clutch all of the scattered raisins as the other children race over to the spot grabbing whatever raisins are in their reach. The teacher calls a halt. To Maria: "You have to share your raisins if you bring them to school . . . but I won't let people grab them from you." She holds the other children back while Maria collects the raisins. Then Maria happily hands out raisins to all the other children and peace returns to the toddler house. Like Paul, she was handing out the raisins on her own terms.

There's something very basic about this. I happily loan my teenage daughters clothing if they ask for it, but I go crazy if they take something without asking, and they betray my trust when they do.

In order to share something, a child first has to possess it . . . really feel the ownership of it.

This issue is a common focus for toddlers because they are just starting to feel their "autonomy," their separateness from other human beings. That is why "no" is such a popular word. Overpowering the child and taking the thing away will produce a scream of outrage, and may prolong the child's learning of the ability to share willingly. Since the attention of toddlers is so easily distracted it's often best to offer the other child a different toy assuring that the first child will share the toy "when he's ready." It helps if you can play with the second child because that adds attractiveness to the second toy. Be sure to praise a child when she is able to finally share the coveted item.

Have Plenty of Toys Available

You *can* redirect toddlers fairly easily and get them interested in a different toy. Don't make your job impossible by having too few toys. Since novelty is an important factor in a toy's appeal, develop a routine of rotating toys, storing them some of the time.

Group Activities

The experience of being part of a group is the first step toward being conscious of the rights of others and developing a social give and take. Singing together, doing finger plays, even sitting at the table and eating together is a step in this direction.

Group Art Activities

Tape a large sheet of paper to the wall or a table top. Let several children scribble or paint on this surface at the same time. This is an experience where children are still "doing their own thing", but are using the same space. They are becoming aware of each other.

Individual Projects, Shared Materials

Try seating two children at a table, giving each his own sheet of paper and putting a common bowl of crayons between them. You can also do this with the large rubber peg boards and put a bowl of pegs between the children. This could be done with other manipulative toys such as Bristle Blocks or other fit together toys or table blocks. You could give each child a tray to work on and put a dish tub of toys between them. This technique usually works very well because there are lots of crayons or toys in the container of things to be shared instead of just one coveted item. The children enjoy the social contact with each other. The teacher can make children conscious of sharing in a positive light. "You two can share these crayons, so you can *both* color."

Pass the Beanbag (Or Anything Else) Game

Boy, is this hard for toddlers! Play music on the record player, and have children pass the beanbag from one to the other while the music is on. When the music stops the child holding the beanbag can do something special, like jump up and down.

Toddlers Always Want the New Thing

No matter how many toys are available, it's always the new one that toddlers want to play with. The newly introduced toy can even be of far less play value or be less attractive than the other toys and still attract attention. Teachers and parents can turn this phenomenon to their advantage.

It is a good idea to "rotate" toys, as suggested several times in this book, putting some away for two weeks or so. When you bring them out again they will be almost like new toys in their appeal to toddlers.

Keep certain toys special for times when you need to occupy children. Many teachers have a "rainy day survival kit" in which they put special toys to bring out only when they would have been outside with children. These things don't have to be expensive or elaborate . . . just *different*. Some possibilities: special dress up clothes such as fancy hats, a feather boa, pretty scarves; stickers, old greeting cards, colored tape; a collection of spray can tops and jar lids for building; a box of pipe cleaners to bend into shapes; perhaps a small flashlight.

A small bag of such things or small inexpensive toys and books from the "dime" store will save your nerves while waiting in the doctor's office, on a long automobile or plane trip, or other times when you must "wait" with your toddler.

Surprise

One of a two year old's favorite words is "surprise". Saying, "I have a surprise for you," is a sure way to get their attention. One teacher brings in a "surprise" each day in a paper grocery sack. It is usually a common household item like rubber gloves or a hand mixer for children to talk about and examine.

Toddlers are Hard to Gather Together

You try to gather children for a story or some group activity. You succeed in getting two or three over to where you want them.

By the time you bring the others over, the first ones are up and gone already. They're like a can of worms!

The "Flop and Do" Technique

Often, it seems, the most effective way to introduce a new activity to toddlers is to simply "flop down" and start doing it. No words of introduction or invitation are usually necessary. Children will simply gravitate over to you. They are "enticed" by your activity and interest rather than compelled by some adult command. This responds to their growing need for "autonomy" to make their own decisions. The children who are developmentally ready and interested in what you're doing will be with you.

Likewise, if you want to generate interest in a toy, just start playing with it yourself. This is a good way to re-interest children in toys that have been around for a while.

Do Special Projects with only a Few Children at a Time

When you do an art project or a cooking project, or anything that requires close supervision, with toddlers it's best to have just 2 or 3 children at a time do it. It's much easier to put on smocks, wipe spills, make the materials available, etc. without causing a lot of wasted "waiting time" for children. Cleaning up is immeasurably easier! Most important, you have a far greater opportunity to provide the "envelope of language" for the experience. You can talk about what each child is doing, and you have time to *listen* and allow the child to talk. It takes you out of the "orchestra conductor" role and puts you into a much more valuable conversational mode with children.

What about the other children?

If you have another adult working with you she or he can play with and supervise the other children. Some teaching teams I know take half the children outside while one teacher remains inside doing a special project with the rest of the group.

If you work alone with a smaller group of children make sure other safe and easy activity choices are available for non-participants, such as puzzles, playdough or fit together toys. You, of course, have to keep one ear open and be able to jump up at a moment's notice.

Often non-participants will want to stand to the side and watch the action. There is nothing wrong with this as long as they have other choices of activities as well. Children can learn a lot by watching others engaged in an activity. It gives them "mental practice" before they do it themselves.

Sometimes children crowd and push and are impatient to participate. This usually happens when this is a new procedure. Simply explaining, "You will have a turn as soon as Billy is finished" is usually sufficient. You could also suggest, "You can stand over here and watch if you want to, or you can play over there and I will call you when it is your turn." Once children gain confidence that they will indeed have a turn the problem usually lessens.

Some teachers worry that some children might not get a chance to do the project if only a few at a time participate. Surprisingly, this is rarely the case. Your preparation and clean-up time is so reduced that there is usually plenty of time for all children who want to do it. You can always repeat the project another time. Ask yourself, "Why am I doing this with children?" If there is any learning value in a project, it's worth doing with a small number of children at a time.

Toddlers Won't Wait

As much as possible, have everything gathered and ready to go before gathering toddlers. Don't invite them to the snack table before the snack is there. Have all the art or cooking project materials in the room and ready before beginning the project, etc.

It's Hard to Keep Toddlers' Attention

Toddlers and twos do have a short and variable attention span. They are also easily distracted. That is another reason why, as previously suggested, you do most things in small groups.

Toddlers have a longer attention span than previously thought to be the case. Their ability to pay attention, like anyone else, will vary based on several factors.

They will be less ready to sit and listen if they are groggy from sleep early in the morning, tired at the end of the day, hungry, or otherwise not feeling tip top. If they are insecure or upset, if they are new to your group, if strangers are in the room, if it was a frantic morning before arriving, if there are distractions such as other children doing something exciting, if there is loud music elsewhere, or a thunderstorm, etc., we cannot expect the concentration of toddlers.

Some hints:

Magic Story Rugs

Collect small carpet samples (free from carpet stores). Place these in a circle on the floor (or in whatever arrangement you want children to be seated.) Seat each child on one carpet sample. This seems to be amazingly helpful in keeping children seated. It defines their own space and there is less kicking and shoving. You can thus make sure each child is in a position where he can see. If you collect a bunch of carpet samples that are all different — in color and/or texture — each child could have her own carpet to sit on day after day. They will quickly learn to identify their own carpet. You can arrange children in advantageous ways by simply placing each child's carpet where you want him to sit.

Animation — Anthropomorphizing

This is the process of giving human-like characteristics to non-human things. This tickles and fascinates young children. It is why so many children's books feature talking animals. Curious George and Frances are examples. It is why puppets have such appeal. *Goodnight Moon,* the book where the child says goodnight to everything in the room, is a true reflection of reality. Young children often talk to chairs, toys, toilets, and the like.

You can take advantage of this phenomenon in your teaching by having inanimate objects talk to the group, telling their life story and social significance. Conjure up a strange voice and hold up a banana and launch into a monologue: "Hello boys and girls. I am a banana. My name is Benny. I have thick yellow skin that's fun to unwrap. See these little brown spots on my tummy — that means I'm ripe and good to eat, etc., etc., etc." (Of course, you might have trouble getting kids to eat Benny once they've made friends with him ... but I doubt it!)

A Pet Puppet

How would you like a classroom assistant who will captivate children at group time, cut your clean up time in half, keep children calm and interested while you're waiting for lunch, help tuck children in at nap time, greet children in the morning, bring out the shy child, help children work out social conflicts and greatly reduce discipline problems?

Skillful use of a "pet puppet" can accomplish all of these things. Although there are many puppets available to buy that would fill the bill, the very best pet puppets are homemade sock puppets. The mouth of a sock puppet opens and closes and its face changes expressions as you move your hand inside, lending extra realism. You can give your pet puppet a real personality with accessories such as hair and eyelashes, a special voice, and of course, a name. He could even wear a name pin. He could have a special "house" (a box or fancy bag) to nap in when not in use.

It is a little disturbing to the ego, but children will pay attention to a puppet much longer than to an adult. He can teach endless concepts during your group time: "Put the ball *under* the chair, *behind* the chair," "Find things in the pile that are *blue*." He or she can organize children at clean up time, help them, and encourage them. You'll be amazed (and perhaps chagrined) at how much eager cooperation children give your puppet! The promise of a special kiss from the puppet and a little one-to-one conversation will get children settled more quickly at nap time. (He sings great lullabyes to individual children, too.)

One teacher I know has a whole army of puppets, all of them specialists. One leads games, one does poetry, one tells stories, one teaches songs, and others entertain at lunch, direct clean up time, etc.

To Make a Basic Sock Puppet:

1. Cut an oval out of cardboard.
2. Glue red felt to one side of the oval and trim.
3. Cut a clean sock across the tip just to where the line across the toes usually comes.

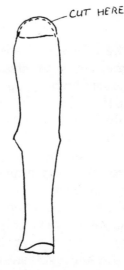

4. Turn the sock inside out.
5. Fold the oval exactly in half.
6. Place the oval in the opening you cut in the sock so the red side is down and the bare cardboard is facing you. Put the corners created by the fold at the ends of the cut in the sock.

7. Stitch around the edges of the oval, through the sock either by hand or with a sewing machine. Do not fold the sock material over the edge of the cardboard — you should have 3 raw edges showing: the cardboard, the felt, and the sock.

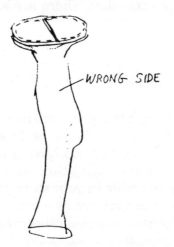

WRONG SIDE

8. Turn the stock back right side out and adjust the material around the mouth. Put your hand inside the puppet to determine where the eyes and other features should go and mark them.

9. Sew on eye buttons, hair, whiskers, ears, etc. whatever you need to give your puppet personality.
10. Give your puppet a name, a voice, and a personality.

Toddlers Don't Like Transitions

Moving toddlers from one place to another can be a job! It's even difficult sometimes to move from one part of your routine to another during the same day. There are some techniques that help.

Consistency of Routine

The most significant thing you can do is to keep your routine consistent from day to day. Young children have only a very vague sense of time, but they do have a sense of the *order* of events. If you always have a story time after snack time, children will automatically assemble in your story place. The order of the particular events doesn't matter as much — just the consistency from day to day. Toddlers are real conservatives. They don't like change.

It also helps to talk about what's going to happen next. "In a few minutes we will go inside and take off our coats. Then we will eat lunch."

Songs for Routines

Music is good for signaling routines. One teacher puts march music on the record player at clean up time. It's fun to make up simple songs to signal various other aspects of your routine such as snack time, clean up time, putting on coats, going inside, lunch, nap, etc. These have the melody cue as well as the words to tell them what to do. For example: (to the tune of "London Bridge")

"Now it's time to have our snack,
Have our snack,
Have our snack,
Now it's time to have our snack,
Come sit down."

Make sure you use different melodies for each song of your routine.

Toddlers Are Afraid of Special Visitors to the Classroom

Research studies have shown that toddlers in day care have significantly less "stranger anxiety" than toddlers cared for at home. They are used to many people coming in and out of the room, and have learned to develop trusting relationships with adults outside of their immediate family. However, child care centers sometimes have costumed characters such as clowns, Santa Claus or the Easter Bunny visit all the children. Although these characters delight older children, they often turn the toddler room upside down.

If you were a new resident on Mars and had just figured out how beings look and act and how the system works, and suddenly something extremely different appeared before you, you'd be scared or at least cautious. That's what's happening when toddlers encounter a costumed character. Who can blame them?

As much as possible, try to prepare your toddlers for the visit before the character comes. Show them pictures of Santa. Talk about how Santa is a nice man who loves children and says, "Ho, ho, ho ..."

When Santa finally arrives, let toddlers approach Santa on their own terms. Don't rush them, don't force them.

If a child is afraid and wants to be held, by all means hold him or her. The child is confirming TRUST in you ... don't pull the rug from under him. Some teachers feel that holding a child who is afraid of Santa or a clown or some other strange visitor is confirming the fear — as though you're agreeing with the child that there really is something to be scared of. This is not the case. What you are really doing is giving the child a secure base from which to venture out. If possible, sit down with the child on your lap and hold him or her loosely so the child can leave your lap whenever she feels ready. You are allowing the child to be in control. You might say, "You can stay right here with me as long as you like. Whenever you feel like it you can get down and go closer."

As you undoubtedly know, once a toddler decides to get off your lap there's no keeping him or her there. Allow the child to be in control and you will lessen the trauma.

Make a judgement call ... you may decide it's best for the character to skip your room.

Toddlers Carry Things Around the Room, Dump Containers Full of Toys and Generally Mess the Place up Quickly

It is true that toddlers like to carry things around. It often doesn't matter what, just so there is something in their hands. And dumping ... well, that's part of their compulsion of emptying and filling containers. These toddler characteristics can be very frustrating to teachers who have set up "interest centers" and like to keep a neat, orderly room.

This is definitely one area where we must not allow adult needs or preferences to overshadow children's needs. That is not to say teachers must let children randomly tear the place apart either.

Organize and simplify your environment. Get a sturdy, labelled container for each toy and designate a special place for each toy to be put away. Frequent pleasant reminders will often get matter-of-fact cooperation. "Put the book back on the shelf, Kevin." You will probably learn to limit the number of toys with many pieces you make available to children each day. If you set these out on a table top rather than just leaving them on a low shelf, children will be more likely to sit down and play with them in a systematic way.

Finally, don't let the mess accumulate all day until it is overwhelming. Designate several clean up times during the day — before snack, before you go outside, before lunch, etc. By all means, invite children's participation in the clean up and express your appreciation for their help. Remember, young children like to put things back into containers almost as much as they like to dump things out.

Some Toddlers Bite When They are Frustrated

"What do you do about biting?" This question has come up at virtually every conference involving toddler care. It is a fairly common problem facing people who provide group care for toddlers. Unfortunately, there is no simple solution.

Why Do Toddlers Bite?

Not *all* toddlers bite other children. Sometimes a toddler classroom will go for months and months without a biting incident and then suddenly there's a "rash" of biting. Since toddlers cannot analyze and explain their actions to us we can only speculate about their motivations.

1. Teething. Toddlers are cutting teeth and it hurts. Chewing on something relieves the itch and makes it feel better. Since there are so many other things to chew on, teething is probably not the only reason toddlers bite other children.
2. Sensory exploration. Toddlers are very efficient at using all of their senses to learn all about the world. They bite *everything* not just their fellow man. The "oral mode", an important style of learning in infancy, is still very strong in toddlers. Both the sense of taste and the sense of touch are rewarded through biting. It feels good to bite! Skin is warm and soft and has a pleasant salty taste. Much to the horror of staff and parents, it is not infrequently the new child who is bitten! Following toddler logic, "Hmmm, I know how she looks ... I know how she smells ... I know how she feels ... I wonder how she tastes and how she sounds when she screams ..." CHOMP!
3. Cause and effect. Toddlers are the scientists of early childhood. They are constantly studying cause and effect. With biting, an action produces a predictable response — and what a response! There's a magnificent noise. Everything in the room comes to a stop. The adult in the room is sure to appear instantly. You are likely to get picked up.
4. Mimicking. This may be why after a long "biteless" period, you suddenly have a bunch of biters! Children learn behaviors

from other children, just like cup banging, waving bye-bye, etc.

5. Self-assertion. This is probably the most common reason toddlers bite. It's a way to express frustration when they don't yet have the language skills to do so. Biting, a child learns, is the quickest and most efficient way to register a protest.

What Can You Do to Prevent or Cut Down on Biting?

One of the most effective techniques for changing behaviors in very young children is redirecting the undesirable behavior to the closest possible parallel activity. Considering the reasons listed of why toddlers bite, think of what other activities you could offer that would satisfy the same urges. Hopefully, you can get toddlers involved in these activities *before* they bite, and dissipate the need.

1. Teething. Keep a bowl of carrot sticks around. Tell a child, "If you need to bite something, tell me, and I'll get you a carrot stick." One teacher keeps small sponges in ziplock bags in the refrigerator for this purpose. Another teacher puts clean wash cloths which were wet and wrung out in the freezer. This requires that you stay alert and perceptive of children's teething distress.

2. Sensory exploration. Give children plenty of opportunities to release tension through "tactile" experiences. Water play is especially soothing. Playdough also allows children to squeeze out tensions. As for the new child, encourage children to come over to her and see her and touch her while you are right there (not all at once, of course). It may help.

3. Cause and effect. There are lots of ways you can allow children to cause legitimate effects on their environment. Of course, if you perceive the effect they're after is to get your attention, that's another matter. The obvious and simplistic answer is to give them more attention. Look at children. Use their names. Smile. Pick them up and waltz with them for no apparent reason.

4. Self-assertion—communicating frustration. Here's the big-
   gie! First, take a good critical look at your program and try to
   cut down on frustration to toddlers. Avoid crowding children.
   Stay within licensing standards for square footage per child,
   and make sure your room arrangement isn't forcing children
   all into one area.

   Allow for autonomy—give children options and many legitimate choices as much as possible. Let them play where they want
   to play. This gives children a feeling of self-control—power—
   and reduces frustration.
   "Head them off at the pass." If you see frustration building in
   a child—grabbing toys or fighting with other children, scream-
   ing, whining, tantrums, etc. redirect the child. Intervene, and get
   them involved in something else.
   Don't require children to share too much. Sharing is an
   unnatural state for toddlers—it is an emerging skill not an
   established skill.
   Work diligently and daily on building children's verbal communication skills—both in giving messages and receiving messages. "Johnny, say 'Stop—don't hit me!' " "Tell her with words
   instead of screams, Jenny. Say, 'I'm using this now.' " "Jason, do
   you hear Jenny? She said 'Mine.' That means she's using that
   now. You can have it when she's through. Here's another puzzle
   you can use."

What Do You Do When Biting Occurs?

   Sometimes classroom conditions can be just fine and children
   will still bite. It just happens—too fast for effective intervention.
   The first thing you have to do, of course, is attend to the victim.
   Put ice on the area immediately. If there is a break in the skin the
   area must be thoroughly cleaned immediately. Depending on the
   severity, it may need attention from a physician.
   Now, dealing with the biter. The trouble is, toddlers don't
   have a sense of the "realness" of other people. They must *learn*
   empathy. Parents often tell staff to bite the child back. Although
   this may convey the message that biting causes pain, it is a

remedy that absolutely cannot be condoned. The real message is that it's okay for adults to hurt people but not for children.

Bring the biter face to face with the victim. Your voice should be angry without yelling. Say to the biter something like: "Biting hurts! Lisa is crying because you hurt her very much! Look at her eyes, there are tears coming out. It's not okay to bite!"

If you can, get the victim to say, "It hurts. I don't want you to bite me!" Research has shown that it's important to give a strong, emphatic, emotional response. Look angry, talk angry, no sweet-talk double messages. Emphasize how it hurts the victim.

Then remove the biter from the spot to the side of the room, separated from the other children. Say, "You have to sit here for a few minutes *until you can play without hurting people!*" As much as possible, try to ignore the biter now. If the biter is getting a lot of your attention as a result of biting, even negative attention, it may reinforce the behavior. Let the child get up after a reasonable time (not longer than 5 minutes) and rejoin the group. "I see you're ready to be with us again." Involve the child in something totally different if possible, something soothing like playdough.

I wish I could tell you that all these words of wisdom will solve all your biting problems, but they may not.

What Do You Do About the Chronic Biter?

If you've tried everything, conferred with parents and used all the approaches you can think of, it may be the time to admit that group care is not the right place for this child *at this time.* Be sure to emphasize to parents that this doesn't mean they have raised a monster! It is a phase that some children go through and all eventually outgrow. Leave the door open for the parent to try the child in your program in another three months or so. In the meantime though, a private sitter may be better for this child. Thus, you are not only protecting the other children, you are doing what is probably best for the child.

The real key to prevent biting in your program is to keep children busy and happy, touch and hug a lot, cut down on toddler frustration, and give children a lot of individual attention. Do what you can to develop empathy in toddlers by describing *feelings* of other children ... all sorts of feelings. Organize with fellow staff so one person's function for a given period is to handle "custodial" matters, diapering, etc. leaving the other staff free to be the "play person", directly involved with the children. Reinforce positive behaviors: "You wanted that doll, Jenny, but you waited for Jason to finish. Good job!" "Good talking, Joe! You used words to tell her what you want."

Turn Your Diapering Area Into a Learning Center

While you're performing the necessary task of changing a toddler's diapers numerous times each day you have the opportunity for some real individual instruction — one to one. Here are a few ideas of ways to take advantage of these short time segments.

1. Hang a mirror on the wall next to the changing counter or attach it securely to the underside of the overhanging shelf if one exists.
2. Play the "Point to your *nose*" game, naming different body parts.
3. Sing nursery rhymes or small songs together or recite simple, rhythmic poems.
4. Choose 3 or 4 vocabulary words a week and put numerous pictures of these on the wall next to your changing area. Then ask the child, "Which one is the motorcycle?" etc.
5. Have some finger puppets there for a child to put on and make talk.
6. Have a bunch of greeting cards, playing cards or pictures covered with clear contact paper to let children hold and talk about.

What else can you think of?

Occupying the child with interesting things to look at and do will make the process go more smoothly. Lots of times toddlers fight and squirm out of boredom. Don't neglect the opportunity for a special hug at this time.

CONCLUSION: "STARTING POINTS"

No book or collection of activities could ever give you all the ideas that might be useful about working with young children.

I challenge you to use the ideas presented in this book as starting points for your own imagination and creative process. Make up your own variations, invent your own toys. Share your ideas and discoveries with others.

I invite you to look at the bibliography and appendix that follow to find more in-depth information on specific topics.

Most of all, I hope you have a wonderful time with the child or children in your care. There is nothing more exciting or more important than watching and participating in the growth of another human being. It is very hard work, but the rewards are immense!

ANNOTATED BIBLIOGRAPHY

There are a great many useful books available about toddlers. This bibliography is certainly not exhaustive, in fact, it barely scratches the surface. I am listing here only my personal favorites which I have found to be most useful.

Books on Child Development

Ames, Louise Bates, and Ilg, Frances L., *Your Two Year Old, Terrible or Tender,* Delacorte Press, 1976.
This book provides very useful insights to the mind of two year olds. There are especially useful and detailed discussions on language development. Aimed at parents, it is non-technical and pragmatic.

Rubin, Richard R., Fisher, John J., and Doering, Susan G., *Your Toddler,* Johnson and Johnson, Child Development Publications. Collier Books. 1980.
This is really 3 books in one. Part One is on growth and development, Part Two on personality and behavior, and Part 3 on play. Part 2 is especially interesting, discussing common toddler problems such as contrariness, temper tantrums, and other special situations.

Stone, Joseph L. and Church, Joseph, *Childhood and Adolescence,* Random House, 1975.
This is the classic college textbook on child development. The first 253 pages are devoted to infant and toddler development.

Then the book goes on to discuss older children up through adolescence, giving the reader a continuum. It's a very interesting book, not dry like many textbooks tend to be. An excellent resource to have on hand.

White, Burton L., *The First Three Years of Life,* Avon, 1978
Burton White has outlined seven phases of development from birth to 36 months of age. For each phase he discusses new abilities and interests of children and suggests ways to maximize a child's potential. I would designate this book essential reading for anyone seriously interested in working with infants and toddlers in a systematic way.

Curriculum Resources

Beginnings—The Magazine for Teachers of Young Children. P.O. Box 2890, Redmond, Wa. 98052.
This quarterly publication goes into depth on a single curriculum topic in each issue, exploring it from all different angles, including infant/toddler curriculum.

Briggs, Dorothy Corkille, *Your Child's Self-Esteem,* Dolphin Books, 1967.
A good guide for developing your parenting style. An in-depth discussion on building a child's self-image.

Cherry, Clare, *Creative Movement for the Developing Child,* Fearon Publishers.

Cromwell, Liz, Hibner, Dixie, *Finger Frolics,* Partner Press, 1976.
Fingerplays for every occasion.

Karnes, Merle B., *You and Your Small Wonder,* American Guidance Service. 1982.
There are many specific activities, each with a 6 month age range assigned to it. There is a useful index of activities according to primary skills emphasized.

Marzollo, Jean, *Supertot,* Harper Colophon Books, 1977.
Fun to read, with hilarious illustrations by Irene Trivas, this book contains many good ideas, activities and toy suggestions.

Matterson, Elizabeth, *Games for the Very Young*, McGraw-Hill, 1969.

This is a collection of finger plays, poems and simple songs.

Mitchell, Grace, *A Very Practical Guide to Discipline*, Telshare Publishing, 1982.

This book describes discipline techniques that work with common problems of children of all ages. Dr. Mitchell draws on a half century of working with children for many lively anecdotes to give the reader understanding about what makes children tick.

Sattler, Helen Roney, *Recipes for Art and Craft Materials*, Lothrop, Lee & Shepard, 1973.

This is a very useful resource for any early education program with all kinds of recipes for pastes, paints, and modelling compounds.

Seeger, Ruth, *American Folk Songs for Children*, Doubleday, 1948.

It contains many simple folk songs and activities to go with them. There is a 48 page introduction explaining how to adapt songs and how to use them with children.

Infant/Toddler Program Design

Cataldo, Christine Z. *Infant and Toddler Programs* — A Guide to Very Early Childhood Education, Addison-Wesley Publishing Company, 1983.

A *very* useful book to anyone wanting to set up or improve a group care program for infants and toddlers. It includes child development information, discussions of equipment and the physical setting, describes teacher and caregiver roles, suggests program activities and describes well-known infant/toddler programs around the country.

Caring for Infants and Toddlers: What Works, What Doesn't, Volumes I and II. Edited by Robert Lurie and Roger Neugebauer, Child Care Information Exchange, 1980, 1982.

These volumes contain distillations of presentations of the yearly conferences of the same name. There are valuable discussions on health and safety, curriculum, discipline, parents, environment, staff training and administration. A very valuable resource.

Supporting the Growth of Infants, Toddlers and Parents, edited by Elizabeth Jones, Pacific Oaks College, Pasadena, Ca. 1979.
This is a collection of essays written by people working in a variety of programs serving infants and toddlers. There is a heavy emphasis on values throughout and would be useful reading for developing program philosophies.

Honig, Alice S., Lally, J. Ronald. *Infant Caregiving,* a design for training, Syracuse University Press, 1981.
The clear focus of this is training people who will work with infants and toddlers in groups. Although there is an emphasis on children under 1, it is applicable to toddler caregiving as well and has some useful exercises.

APPENDIX

Early Childhood Toy and Equipment Suppliers (send for catalogues)

Beckley-Cardy   (general)
7500 Old Oak Road
Middleburg Heights, Ohio 44130

Childcraft Education Corporation   (general)
20 Kilmer Road
Edison, N.J. 08818

Community Playthings   (wooden toys and furniture)
Rifton, N.Y. 12471

Constructive Playthings   (general)
2008 West 103rd Terrace
Leawood, Kansas

Kaplan School Supply Corporation   (general)
600 Jonestown Road
Winston-Salem, N.C. 27103

Learning Products, Inc.   (specialized plastic toys)
11632 Fairgrove Industrial Blvd.
St. Louis, Mo. 63043

Gryphon House, Inc.   (quality children's literature
                            and teacher resource books)
3706 Otis Street, P.O. Box 275
Mt. Rainier, Md. 20712

Conferences and Seminars

Caring for Infants and Toddlers — What Works, What Doesn't?

This is typically a 2 day conference meeting in the spring

each year in Summit, N.J. and San Francisco. There is a diverse group of presentors representing many types of programs and providing a broad expertise. The focus is putting together a quality child care program. For information write:

> Robert Lurie, Executive Director
> Summit Child Care Center
> 14 Beekman Terrace
> Summit, N.J. 07901

Educating the Infant and Toddler

This is a 2 day institute presented by Dr. Burton White, offered in response to a dramatic rise in professional activities in the field of infant education and well-being. Dr. White provides participants with a wealth of information in 2 days of lecture and video tapes, providing a grounding in sound child development understandings. These institutes are presented in cities all over the country on an on-going basis. For information write:

> The Center for Parent Education
> 55 Chapel Street
> Newton, Mass. 02160

Quality Infant/Toddler Caregiving Workshop

Dr. Alice Honig presents this week long summer intensive study program at Syracuse University in New York. There is an examination of current research pertinent to infants and toddlers. It is a combination of lectures, movies, reading and interacting with real babies. For information write:

> Syracuse University
> College for Human Development
> 200 Slocum Hall
> Syracuse, N.Y. 13210

Index

Must Reading For Early Childhood Educators